From Reconstruction to Revolution:

The Blacks' Struggle for Equality

THE WHIPPING-POST.
HUNTED DOWN WITH BLOOD-HOUNDS.
SLAVERY FOR YEARS.
BRANDED AND MANAULED.
THE AUCTION BLOCK—HUSBAND AND WIFE, PARENT AND CHILD, BROTHER AND SISTER SOLD APART.
DAUGHTERS, MOTHERS, WIVES, AND SISTERS RUINED.
KNOWLEDGE A SEALED BOOK.
FORT PILLOW MASSACRE.
"*Resolved by the Congress of the Confederate States of America*, That the thanks of Congress are due and are hereby cordially tendered to Major-General FORREST and other officers and men of his command, for their late brilliant and successful campaign in Mississippi, West Tennessee, and Kentucky—a campaign which has conferred on its authors fame as enduring as the records of the struggle which they have so brilliantly illustrated."
NO QUARTER TO THE "NIGGER!"
NEW YORK RIOTS—BURNING OF THE COLORED ORPHAN ASYLUM; LAMP-POST GALLOWS.
HOMES BURNED.
NEW ORLEANS AND MEMPHIS MASSACRES.
"A NEGRO HAS NO RIGHTS WHICH A WHITE MAN IS BOUND TO RESPECT."
"THIS IS A WHITE MAN'S GOVERNMENT."
"The nigger and the white man are not likely to agree, unless the nigger yields to the white man's views, which he can do, or die."—*The Jefferson* (Texas).
"We must make the negro understand we are the men we were when we held them in abject bondage."—*Meridian* (Miss.) *Mercury*.
"Agree among yourselves, and act firmly on this agreement, that you will not employ any one who votes the Radical ticket."—WADE HAMPTON.
"And now I say that, unless the negroes submit to the intelligent guidance of the powerful white race, their fate will be that of the Indians: they will be exterminated. The negroes can only be happy and prosperous as long as they are guided by the intelligence of the white race. Whenever it is sought to disfranchise the intelligence of the country, and make it subordinate to the ignorance of the country; whenever it is sought to subordinate the white race of the country to the black barbarism of the negro, the prosperity of the country is at an end."—BLAIR.
"We are bound to have a war of races, and when there is one drop of blood spilled, we predict that it will flow as freely as does the Mississippi."—*The Jefferson* (Texas).
BULLETS—REBEL PROTESTS AGAINST REPUBLICAN MEETINGS; CAMILLA, GEORGIA. KU-KLUX KLAN.
NEGRO KILLED—"ONE VOTE LESS."—*Richmond Whig*.
EXPULSION OF COLORED MEMBERS OF THE HOUSE OF REPRESENTATIVES IN GEORGIA.
EXPELLED FROM THE JURY BOX.
FORCED AWAY FROM THE POLLS.
BURNING SCHOOL-HOUSES AND CHURCHES THROUGHOUT THE "RECONSTRUCTED STATES."
HUNG UP OR SHOT DOWN IN THE ROADS AND STREETS.
"COLORED CRIMINALS SUFFER SEVERER PUNISHMENT THAN WHITES GUILTY OF THE SAME CRIMES."
THE GEORGIA MASSACRE.
"WE DESPISE THE NEGRO."—*N. Y. World*.
COLORED
ORPHAN
FREEDMAN SCHOOL
Th: Nast

From Reconstruction to Revolution:

The Blacks' Struggle for Equality

Joseph A. Alvarez

Atheneum 1971 New York

Copyright © 1971 by Joseph A. Alvarez
All rights reserved
Library of Congress catalog card number 78-154747
Published simultaneously in Canada by McClelland & Stewart, Ltd.
Manufactured in the United States of America
by Halliday Lithograph Corporation
West Hanover, Massachusetts
First Edition

For My Mother and My Father

CONTENTS

Out of Their Old Relation	3
Reconstruction	16
The Radicals: Prophets Without Honor	18
Reconstruction in Black and White	35
The Jim Crow Era	50
Black Awakening	74
Revolution	102
The Fight to Integrate	104
The Twilight of Nonviolence	132
Black Nationalism	163
Rebellion in the Ghetto	183
BIBLIOGRAPHICAL NOTE	208

From Reconstruction to Revolution:

The Blacks' Struggle for Equality

The problem of the twentieth century is the problem of the color line, the relation of the darker to the lighter races of men in Asia and Africa, in America and the islands of the sea.

W.E.B. Du Bois, 1903

"I don't know as I 'spected nothing from freedom . . ."
South Carolina Freedman

OUT OF THEIR OLD RELATION

April 9, 1865. Palm Sunday. As Christians in their churches commemorated Jesus' triumphant entry into Jerusalem, a solemn group of army officers played out quite a different ritual in the hushed village of Appomattox, Virginia. Four years of war—and beyond that, 200 years of slavery—lay behind the soldiers' hastily convened meeting. Gathered in the musty parlor of Wilmer McLean's tree-shaded farmhouse, they muted the bitterness of the occasion with polite reminiscences of happier times before the war, when they had been comrades-in-arms instead of adversaries. Outside, the officers' horses nibbled at the spring grass under the watchful eyes of orderlies.

"The terms I propose," said Ulysses S. Grant finally, "are those stated substantially in my letter of yesterday—that is, the officers and men surrendered to be paroled and disqualified from taking up arms again until properly exchanged, and all arms, ammunition and supplies to be delivered up as captured property."

"Those," replied Robert E. Lee, "are about the conditions I expected would be proposed."

Grant wrote out the terms; Lee read them and signed his acceptance. A shaking of hands all around, and it was over. The War of the Rebellion, the bloodiest conflict in American history, was ended.

Three days later, under gray, threatening skies, the remnants of Lee's army formally surrendered their arms. Marching in close order, they filed down the main street of Appomattox between two long lines of blue-uniformed troops. Halting at the end of the Union gauntlet, the Confederates stacked their rifles, cartridge boxes and battle flags and moved on.

No cannon saluted victory; no drums rolled defeat. Lee was there, but Grant already had left for Washington. Grant's designated representative, General J. L. Chamberlain, reviewed the traditional ceremony in awed silence, "as if it were the passing of the dead," he later wrote.

There was good cause for restraint. More than 620,000 Americans had died, at least another 375,000 had suffered wounds. Slavery, the root of the rebellion, had been abolished, but the attitudes that slavery had bred remained. After two hundred years, they could not be expected to vanish overnight.

The white man—whether English, German, Italian or Irish—had found freedom in America. And with freedom came hope and opportunity. The black man, however, had come to America in chains. Wrested from his home and sold into slavery in an alien land, he was *property* for 200 years.

Slavery itself was not new, of course. It dates back to the rise of the earliest agricultural civilizations in Egypt, Asia and the Middle East. Ancient Egyptians, Romans and Greeks both held and were slaves. But the basis of most ancient slavery was war—if your side lost, you were a slave; if it won, you were a slaveholder. It remained for the African slave trade to base slavery on racial inferiority, and for western "civilization" and Christian apologists to justify it.

Only in America was the slave judged inferior because of his color. In their ignorance, Americans considered the black man uncivilized. Unaware that some black African civilizations predated theirs by a thousand years and more, they thought the African a primitive brute to be used like a horse or trained like a dog. They deprived him of almost every human dignity—a secure family life, privacy, even a name and the knowledge of his birthday. Beneath the ignorance, behind the injustices and cruelty, lay racism—the belief that one race is superior to another. And while slavery was an institution peculiar to the South, racism was not. "The prejudice of race," wrote the French aristocrat, Alexis de Tocqueville, who visited the United States in 1831, "appears to be stronger in the states that have abolished slavery than in those where it still exists; and nowhere is it so intolerant as in those states where servitude has never been known." Furthermore, de Tocqueville noted, "the prejudice which repels the Negroes seems to increase in proportion as they are emancipated, and inequality is sanctioned by the manners while it is effaced from the laws of the country."

These were the problems that both whites and blacks had to face. The white man would have to see the black man as a person. And the black man, having won his freedom, now would have to win equality. As the writer and poet, James Weldon Johnson, said many years later, the race question involved "the saving of black America's body and white America's soul." Appomattox was the first step in a long journey still unfinished.

* * *

The triumph of northern arms released from bondage four million blacks. Legally, however, these people had no rights, not even the basic right of citizenship. And without rights, without land or jobs, education or opportunity, without even food or shelter in many instances, what was freedom?

"I don't know as I 'spected nothing from freedom," said a typical South Carolina freedman, "but they turned us out like a bunch of stray dogs. No homes, no clothing, no nothing, not enough food to last us one meal. . . . All we had to farm with was sharp sticks. We'd stick holes and plant corn, and when it came up we'd punch up the dirt round it. We didn't plant cotton, 'cause we couldn't eat that."

The white southerner had his own wounds to lick. Artillery and arson had razed his cities and towns, neglect had withered his crops, the army had commandeered his livestock, the Union blockade had throttled his commerce, violence and frustration had seared his spirit. He was living off the dregs of defeat. Bands of ragged, starving men drifted home from the battlefields, begging and looting what scraps of food and stores remained in cellars and smokehouses throughout the countryside. "The props that held society up are broken," a Georgia girl noted in her diary. "Everything is in a state of disorganization and tumult. We have no currency, no law save the primitive code that might makes right. . . . The suspense and anxiety in which we live are terrible."

In Mississippi, in Alabama, in Texas, in the Carolinas, the situation was the same: the old order had crumbled, leaving a cloud of apprehension hanging over the ruins. The sectional struggle now moved from the battlefield to Washington; military tactics gave way to political maneuvering. What would be the black man's role in the new

Ruins of the Gallego Flour Mills, Richmond, Virginia, burned during the evacuation of Richmond April 23, 1865. Photograph by Mathew Brady, 1865. Collection The Museum of Modern Art, New York.

order? That was the question that lay beneath the private agony and the public rhetoric of reconstruction.

The black man himself wanted land—"forty acres and a mule." Not even the ballot meant so much to him, for land gave his freedom substance; it was tangible, he could cultivate it, build on it, sift it through his fingers. Land was, indeed, the third of the three props of American society—life, freedom, property—which the Founding Fathers had adopted from John Locke, the 17th century English social philosopher. The black man knew nothing about Locke, but he intuitively understood the importance of property. "Give us our own land and we take care of ourselves," said one, expressing the sentiment of the mass of freedmen.

This philosophy was put to work in 1865 in South Carolina and Mississippi. On the fertile sea islands around Port Royal, South Carolina, federal authorities sold or rented abandoned and confiscated land to more than 30,000 freedmen. And in Davis Bend, Mississippi, the government divided the acreage of six large plantations (including Jefferson Davis') among 1,800 freedmen. The former slaves proved to be excellent free farmers. Those at Davis Bend, for example, after repaying all loans, showed a cash profit of $159,200 at the end of the year.

"A wiser and more benevolent government," wrote historian Vernon L. Wharton, "might well have seen in Davis Bend the suggestion of a long-time program for making the Negro a self-reliant, prosperous and enterprising element of the population." But it didn't, and in its shortsightedness the government probably reflected the apathy of the majority of people, North and South. Americans, having just quelled a political rebellion, were unwilling to endure the social revolution that land reform would have triggered.

Such an attitude had a long history. Abraham Lincoln, sensing it, declined to press for land reform in the South under the so-called Second Confiscation Act of 1862. The Act defined rebellion or insurrection as a crime punishable by fine, imprisonment and confiscation of property (including slaves). Had it been utilized as its sponsors intended, it might have changed the lives of dispossessed southerners of both races. But Lincoln first forced Congress to limit the confiscation of land to the lifetime of the owner; then, he pointedly neglected to enforce the measure; finally, through executive amnesty, he exempted most southerners from the law's penalties.

It is ironic that Lincoln, who couldn't himself decide what to do with the black man, should block the most promising program for integrating him into white America. But Lincoln was a politician, not a reformer, and the role of the "Great Emancipator" was not one he chose. "I am not, nor ever have been, in favor of bringing about in any way the social and political equality of the white and black races," he said, debating Stephen A. Douglas in 1858. This was not only a politically expedient position to take in an Illinois senatorial race, but a sincere expression of Lincoln's convictions. "President Lincoln was a white man, and shared the prejudices common to his countrymen towards the colored race," Frederick Douglass, the militant black abolitionist, once observed. "Viewed from the genuine abolition ground, Mr. Lincoln seemed tardy, cold, dull and indifferent; but measuring him by the sentiment of his country, a sentiment he was bound as a statesman to consult, he was swift, zealous, radical and determined."

Lincoln favored a gradual, compensated emancipation that would stretch out to the twentieth century. This plan, he explained to Congress in 1862, would spare "both races from the evil of sudden derangement" and ease the anguish of the militant slavers, most of whom would be dead by 1900. Once emancipated, the blacks would be sent to colonies in Africa, South America and the Caribbean islands. Congress even appropriated $600,000 to experiment with colonization.

On New Year's Day, 1863, Lincoln issued his Emancipation Proclamation. Although it has been acclaimed as a great document, it was in reality little more than wartime propaganda. "That proclamation frees the slave but ignores the Negro," commented abolitionist Wendell Phillips at the time. In fact, it didn't even free the slaves. Lincoln's order applied only to the rebellious southern states (where the government exercised no authority) and specifically exempted federally controlled territory. The London *Spectator* suggested tartly that the principle behind the President's edict "is not that a human being cannot justly own another but that he cannot own him unless he is loyal to the United States."

Emancipation, then, was not complete until the adoption of the Thirteenth Amendment, abolishing slavery, in 1865. Lincoln, of course, supported the Amendment. By that time he was grappling with the problem of reconstruction, which he saw as returning the southern states to "their proper practical relation with the Union" as quickly as possible.

Lincoln believed this was a presidential task. "I think it providential," he told his Cabinet after Appomattox, "that this great rebellion is crushed just as Congress has adjourned and there are none of the disturbing elements [the so-called radicals] of that body to hinder and embarrass us. If we are wise and discreet we shall reanimate the states and get their governments in successful operation, with order prevailing and the Union reestablished, before Congress comes together in December."

The President already had moved toward this goal. In 1863 he had proclaimed a reconstruction policy under which he would recognize a state government organized by as little as ten percent of the eligible voters of 1860, when that many had taken a loyalty oath to the Union. The new government had to accept only emancipation of blacks; it did not have to grant them any rights. Lincoln suggested giving the ballot to black soldiers and to "the very intelligent." But he made it clear that this was only a suggestion, and when Louisiana, Arkansas and Tennessee ignored it, he did not refuse them recognition. Indeed, 19 of the 25 Union states denied blacks the ballot, and the white voter seemed determined to keep it that way. Shortly after the war, the people of Connecticut, Kansas, Michigan, Minnesota and Ohio rejected proposals for black suffrage.

This was Lincoln's idea of reconstruction, but the Republicans in Congress—particularly the radical faction—had insisted on a voice in any postwar program. The radicals, a coalition of abolitionists, reformers, militants and laissez-faire expansionists, were committed to black equality and suppression of white southern power. "If all whites must vote, then must all blacks," insisted Massachusetts Senator Charles Sumner. And in the House, Thaddeus Stevens of Pennsylvania demanded "a radical reorganization of southern institutions, habits and manners."

In 1864 Senator Benjamin F. Wade of Ohio and Representative Henry W. Davis of Maryland, dissatisfied with the President's "ten percent plan," steered a radical reconstruction bill through Congress. Under it, each southern state would be ruled by a military governor, one of whose duties would be to supervise voter enrollment. At least half of the enrolled voters would have to take a loyalty oath. From these ranks delegates to a new constitutional convention would be elected. The delegates would have to take a second oath that they never had voluntarily supported the Confederacy, and the convention would have to repudiate secession and abolish slavery. Black suffrage, however, was not mentioned.

Lincoln pocket-vetoed the Wade–Davis bill, explaining that he did not wish to be "inflexibly committed to any single plan of restoration." Wade and Davis responded to Lincoln's veto with an irate "manifesto." The President, they insisted, should "confine himself to his executive duties . . . and leave political reorganization to Congress."

Lincoln, however, was not a man to turn his back on political opportunity. And reconstruction promised to provide unparalleled political opportunity. The Confederacy was predominantly Democratic; but defeat, Lincoln realized, would create a political vacuum in the South. As a loyal party man, he wanted to fill that vacuum with Republicans.

It may have seemed irrational of Lincoln to want to plant the Republican seed in the South, where the party's antislavery principles had made it anathema. But Lincoln was a special kind of Republican, a former Whig, and he hoped to draw the former southern Whigs to the Republican fold.

The Whig coalition—it could not be called a party— had formed in the 1830's to oppose the new popular democracy in general and Andrew Jackson, its symbol, in particular. It included nationalists like Henry Clay (Lincoln's hero), states' righters like John Tyler, rabid slavers like John Calhoun, and antislavers like William Seward. Twice the Whigs had finessed a military hero into the White House—William Henry Harrison in 1840 and Zachary Taylor in 1848. Both men died in office, leaving their duties to their Vice-Presidents, John Tyler, a Virginia planter, and Millard Fillmore, a Buffalo backwoodsman. Fillmore made possible Henry Clay's historic Compromise of 1850, in which California was admitted to the Union as a free state in exchange for a stringent fugitive slave law. Ironically, the Compromise—which satisfied no one—had proved to be the death of the Whig coalition. The slavery debate heated up, and in 1854 the coalition disintegrated. Antislavers and nationalists formed the Republican Party; slavers and states' righters drifted into the Democratic Party or into isolated third-party movements.

Lincoln believed that the Republican party was the true

heir of Whig conservatism. With the divisive issue of slavery resolved, he planned to woo the southern conservatives and lead his party out of the sectionalism to which the war had bound it.

It was a delicate task. He could not manage it by advocating black suffrage. Nor could he do it by imposing upon the South the severe reconstruction that the radicals favored. But he also knew he could not disregard the demands of the Republicans in Congress. Lincoln pondered alternatives.

The ticklish problem was the disposition of the freedmen. What could he do with the blacks that would be fair to them yet not odious to the whites? In 1865 he still favored colonization, but that idea seemed doomed. "I suppose one of the principal difficulties in the way of colonization," he admitted, "is that the free colored man cannot see that his comfort would be advanced by it."

Sending up trial balloons, Lincoln talked about "temporary arrangements for the freed people." He outlined a program of apprenticeship "by which the two races could gradually live themselves out of their old relation to each other, and both come out better prepared for the new."

While Lincoln pondered, blacks, themselves, were understandably wary of what the future might hold. Frederick Douglass expressed their concern at a victory celebration in Boston's famous Faneuil Hall. Noting that one of the speakers had addressed the scattered blacks in the audience as "fellow citizens," Douglass reminded the white listeners that blacks seemed to be citizens only in times of national crisis. They had served—and with distinction—in every American war, including the one just concluded. Now, insisted Douglass, the black man "must also be a citizen in time of peace. He must have the right to vote."

Like the masterful politician that he was, Lincoln remained flexible. Before Congress adjourned, administration supporters had introduced a bill to readmit Louisiana to the Union under the President's ten percent plan. Senator Sumner went straight to the White House. "Mr. President," he said firmly, "this bill ought not to pass, and it shall not pass." And it didn't. But Lincoln publicly minimized his disagreement with Sumner and the radicals as "one of mere form and little else," and he acknowledged his own responsibility in "the duty of harmony between Congress and the Executive."

Sumner and Lincoln began working toward a settlement of their differences. Two days after Appomattox, in a speech at a victory celebration, Lincoln hinted at a possible compromise.

A crowd had gathered on the White House lawn to hear the speech. The evening dampness that drifted over from the nearby Potomac River was ignored as bands played patriotic songs and the people cheered, waved banners and generally frolicked. Lincoln appeared on the second floor balcony, and the crowd roared its affection. Finally, the cheering subsided and the President began a prepared speech.

"Fellow citizens," he said, reading by the light of a candle held by a reporter, "we meet this evening not in sorrow but in gladness of heart. The evacuation of Petersburg and Richmond, and the surrender of the principal insurgent army, give hope of a righteous and speedy peace, whose joyous expression cannot be restrained." More cheers. Lincoln waited, then read on, explaining his plan for the readmission of Louisiana to the Union. "Concede that the new government of Louisiana is only to what it should be as the egg is to the fowl," he said, "we shall sooner have the fowl by hatching the egg than by smashing it."

As Lincoln finished reading each page of the speech, he let it flutter to the floor, where his son Tad gathered it up. Finally, after noting that "no exclusive and inflexible plan can safely be prescribed," he concluded by saying: "In the present situation, as the phrase goes, it may be my duty to make some new announcement to the people of the South. I am considering, and shall not fail to act, when satisfied that action will be proper."

Perhaps Sumner already had agreed to yield on Louisiana if Lincoln would guarantee protection of the freedmen's rights in the other southern states. We shall never know. But in a Cabinet meeting three days after his speech, the President again appeared ready to compromise. Stanton presented a plan—which Sumner must have known about—for the military occupation of the South as the first step toward reconstruction. Lincoln neither endorsed nor rejected it; instead he urged Stanton to "revise" it in time for further discussion at the next Cabinet meeting.

But for Lincoln the next Cabinet meeting never came. He was assassinated that evening at Ford's theater by actor John Wilkes Booth, a fanatic southern sympathizer. The problems of reconstruction fell to Vice-President Andrew Johnson, a Unionist, a Democrat, a southerner.

Reconstruction

Lincoln, and Johnson after him, favored reconstruction plans with a minimum of federal interference in the affairs of the former Confederate states. Before he died, Lincoln had approved such a plan for Louisiana. Once in office, Johnson immediately approved a similar plan for the other southern states.

But Republicans in Congress, particularly the radicals, had other ideas. Disturbed by continued oppression of the black man in the South, they nullified presidential reconstruction and undertook the task themselves. In 1866 Congress passed the first Civil Rights Act—over Johnson's veto. A year later, it passed the First Reconstruction Act—also over the President's veto. In 1868 Congress approved the Fourteenth Amendment and the states—including some southern states which by then had been reconstructed under the 1867 Reconstruction Act—ratified it. Two years later, the Fifteenth Amendment was similarly adopted.

17 RECONSTRUCTION

By mid-1870, all the former Confederate states had been reconstructed under the congressional plan. But almost as soon as they were reconstructed, they began to be "redeemed" by southern conservatives. Eight of the eleven southern states had been redeemed by the end of 1875. That same year Congress passed a broad Civil Rights Act. But it proved to be a token gesture. Two years later, in 1877, with the certification of Rutherford B. Hayes as President, reconstruction came to an end and rigorous repression of the black man began anew.

"The real trouble is that *we hate the Negro.*"
Radical Congressman
George W. Julian of Indiana

THE RADICALS: PROPHETS WITHOUT HONOR

Less than three hours after Lincoln's death, Andrew Johnson, a onetime tailor's apprentice, took the oath as 17th President of the United States. The new President, the radical leaders believed, would adopt a stronger reconstruction policy than the conservative Lincoln had. As Vice-President, Johnson frequently had voiced his conviction that "treason must be made odious and traitors must be punished and impoverished."

The radicals were confident that Johnson would cooperate with them as Lincoln had not. Sumner, after several visits with the new President, described his expectations in a letter to a friend:

"I said during this winter that the rebel states should not come back except on the footing of the Declaration of Independence and the complete recognition of human rights. I feel more than ever confident that all this will be fulfilled. And then what a regenerated land! I had looked for a bitter contest on this question; but with the President on our side, it will be carried by simple avoirdupois."

Clearly, it was the Republicans who would create reconstruction. With comfortable majorities in the House and the Senate, the Republicans were firmly in control of Congress. They were, however, divided among themselves over the form and the extent of reconstruction. A small band of conservatives, dedicated to rocking the ship of state as little as possible, favored the late President's general approach. The moderates, the largest group, were sympathetic to the Lincolnian approach, but they wanted a voice in reconstruction and were willing to go further than Lincoln had gone in changing southern institutions. Holding the balance of power, they waited for Johnson to declare himself.

The radicals were weaker than the moderates but stronger than the conservatives. "Radical" means "to go to the root of," and these men wished to reconstruct southern society fundamentally, in Stevens' words, "to overcome the prejudice and ignorance and wickedness" that denied blacks equality before the law.

Most traditional historians maintain that the radicals' moral fervor was largely a guise; that their real interests were in gaining economic advantages for northern industrialists and political power for themselves. It is a question of degree. The radicals certainly were motivated by economic and political as well as humanitarian considerations; in politics there are no pure motives. Some modern historians, however, have shown that idealism was as strong among the radicals as it was among the abolitionists —many of whom, indeed, were radicals. They often worked hand in hand.

Characteristic of the radical abolitionists was the Boston patrician, Wendell Phillips. With William Lloyd Garrison's retirement from the antislavery movement in 1865 (he thought his work was completed), Phillips became the foremost spokesman for those white Americans who objected to racism on moral grounds. He also crusaded for women's suffrage, temperance, humane treatment of the insane, a graduated income tax, an eight-hour work day and the right of workers to strike. Tall, cool, with a piercing eye and wit, Phillips was perhaps the most gifted orator of his time. His life was little more than a long series of public agitations. But his facility with language and ideas, and his inexorable idealism, gave him, in the words of a contemporary correspondent, "as great an influence on political affairs as any man can have who is outside of political organization. . . ."

In the political arena, the radicals were led by Senator Charles Sumner of Massachusetts and Congressman Thaddeus Stevens of Pennsylvania.

Sumner, another passionate reformer, had advocated women's suffrage, prison reform and temperance, as well as abolition. Aristocratic in bearing, fastidious in dress and manner, he was seen by one contemporary as a man of "large qualities and small defects." One of these defects was vanity. Someone once remarked to General Grant that Sumner placed no faith in the Bible. "No, he didn't write it," Grant replied, in one of his rare flashes of wit.

He was not a man to compromise. "I had hoped that the day of compromise with wrong had passed forever," he said of the question of the black man's rights. "Ample experience shows that it is the least practical mode of settling questions involving moral principles. A moral principle cannot be compromised."

Stevens was more complex. Personally ambitious and politically shrewd, he watched over the interests of northern manufacturing and railroads as well as those of the black man. He was a gaunt, rugged bachelor with a taste for gambling and for ladies and a flair for the dramatic. As an old man he once was stopped by a lady who asked for a lock of his hair. "Please, madame, take it all," he said, handing her the wig he was wearing.

Like Sumner, Stevens was a dedicated advocate of black equality. "Every man," he insisted, "no matter what his race or color . . . has an equal right to justice, honesty and fair play with every other man; and the law should secure him those rights." Even in death Stevens was implacable. His will directed that he be buried in a black cemetery to protest the common practice of excluding blacks from white burial grounds.

In sympathy with the radicals, and one of the most effective spokesmen for their views, was the great black abolitionist, Frederick Douglass. Born a slave in 1817, Douglass had endured hunger, privation and humiliation, casual cruelty and brutality bred by the slave system, before escaping from bondage in 1838. He had learned to read from the pages of books and newspapers scavenged from the gutters of Baltimore, and he had taught himself to write by copying the names from the prows of the vessels in the shipyard where he worked. Once he reached the North, Douglass became a brilliant lecturer and writer for the abolitionist movement and a dedicated advocate of equal rights for all men. "The fundamental and everlasting objection to slavery," he insisted, "is not that it sinks a Negro to the condition of a brute but that it sinks a *man* to that condition."

Few American lives have been spent so relentlessly as Douglass's in the service of the principles enunciated in the Declaration of Independence, that are supposed to be the foundation of the American republic. At a time when few others would step forward, Douglass vigorously supported women's suffrage and protested against capital punishment and the systematic oppression of American Indians and Chinese immigrants.

He put himself on the firing line. On one occasion his arm was broken by a hostile audience, and only a timely rescue by a friend saved his life. One of the first of the "freedom riders," Douglass made a point of sitting in the "white" coaches of segregated trains. "I was often dragged out of my seat, beaten and severely bruised by conductors and brakemen," he reported. One such incident in Massachusetts so dramatized the injustice of segregated trains that the railroad ended the practice.

Douglass was 48 years old when the Civil War ended. The foremost black leader, he was an American celebrity and an internationally renowned reformer. At first he considered retiring from public life, but he soon realized that his talents still were needed. "Slavery is not abolished until the black man has the ballot," he told the members of the American Antislavery Society in a debate over whether or not to disband. And in speech after speech he elaborated upon this theme.

His fears were not ill-founded. On May 29, 1865, six weeks after his succession to the presidency, Johnson revealed his reconstruction policy in two proclamations.

The first one granted amnesty and restored "all rights of property except as to slaves" to southerners who took an oath of allegiance to the United States. Former Confederate officers and officials and wealthy planters were excluded. They had to apply for special executive pardons; but they were promised—and they received—a sympathetic hearing.

The second proclamation listed the conditions for reorganizing the government of North Carolina. Setting the pattern for reorganization throughout the South, it required the state to abolish slavery and to repudiate secession and war debts but left to it the determination of the freedman's political and civil rights, including, of course, the right to vote. Few people doubted how the southern states would handle black suffrage; and predictably, all eleven of them denied blacks the ballot.

Those blacks who were able to organize protested this betrayal. In October, 1865, a group of Mississippians, speaking for the mass of freedmen who "owing to the prejudice existing" in the state had "not been able to assemble in convention," petitioned Congress for the right to vote. "As we have fought in favor of liberty, justice and humanity," they stated, "we wish to vote in favor of it and give our influence to the permanent establishment of pure republican institutions in these United States."

Eight southern states also enacted discriminatory "Black Codes." These laws established the black man's right to marry and to hold property, but they severely restricted his choice of work and his right to move around freely. Blacks without jobs could be arrested for vagrancy, after which they could be hired out to work off their jail sentences—their former masters getting first call on their labor.

This was reconstruction in the spirit of Lincoln's ten percent plan, which Congress had rejected in 1863. "The reconstruction of rebel states without Negro suffrage is a practical surrender to the Confederacy," cried Wendell Phillips. But Johnson himself described his policy as "restoration," not reconstruction. He quickly recognized restored governments in Louisiana, Arkansas, Virginia and Tennessee and issued proclamations for the restoration of the remaining Confederate states. Mississippi held its constitutional convention in mid-August; the Carolinas, Alabama, Georgia and Florida rapidly followed suit. By December, when Congress reconvened, only Texas remained outside the Johnson fold, and it would come around the following April.

This was not what the radicals had expected. From their helpless position, with Congress not in session they asked each other what had caused Johnson's turnaround. A closer look at his past, however, would have shown them that his actions were consistent with his background.

Born in 1808, Johnson had begun life in Raleigh, North Carolina, where a man's origin defined the limits of his social acceptance, and his color defined the limits of his freedom. As the second son of poor, landless whites, he was free but socially unacceptable to the agrarian aristocrats who reigned over southern society. When Johnson was three his father died; from then until he was a grown man, he "wrestled with poverty," as he put it. At fourteen he was bound as an apprentice to a tailor. Two years later he ran away to escape "persecution" for a youthful prank. After some wandering he returned to Raleigh and with his family set out for the hill country of East Tennessee, settling in Greenville, the county seat of a region of small farms and few slaves. The frontier spirit still lingered in East Tennessee. Johnson was accepted there. Within a few months he had his own tailor shop and an attractive young wife, Eliza McCardle.

The new Mrs. Johnson taught her husband to read and write. Eager to be somebody, Johnson studied diligently and worked long hours. In a more congenial atmosphere, and with a formal education, he might have become a teacher. Instead, he plunged into Tennessee politics. Campaigning as a champion of the working man, he was elected alderman of Greenville in 1828 at the age of twenty. A slashing, flamboyant stump speaker, he went from alderman to mayor to the state legislature and to Congress in rapid succession. Gerrymandered out of Congress, Johnson ran for governor of Tennessee and won two terms. "The new Andy Jackson," people called him. He was for the shopkeeper and the yeoman farmer, against northern capitalists and southern planters. "The people need friends," he said, "they have a great deal to bear."

In 1857 he went to the United States Senate where he watched the Union dissolved. By then a slave owner himself, Johnson was opposed more to secession than to slavery; he saw that one would not survive the other. In 1860, when the Union was threatened, he told his secessionist friends: "If you persist in forcing the issue . . . against the government, I say in the face of Heaven, give me my government and let the Negro go." He was the only southern senator to remain loyal to the United States.

Marked for death in his own state, Johnson narrowly escaped to the North. Lincoln, grateful to have with him a loyal southerner from a border state, appointed Johnson military governor of Tennessee in 1862. Two years later he made him his running mate, even though Johnson was a Democrat.

Some Republicans had been wary of putting a southern Democrat, even a proven Unionist, into the vice-presidency. Their fears were vindicated when President Johnson, locked into middle-class attitudes by his background and experiences, and sharing the white man's low opinion of the black man's capabilities, could not see that federal muscle was needed to keep the blacks from being returned to slavery in fact if not in name. He argued that civil rights and voting qualifications were matters of state, not federal, jurisdiction. "I was born a states' rights Democrat and I shall die one," he said. His politics can be summed up in those twelve words.

Southern leaders who flocked to Washington to plead

for pardons subtly made the President their captive. Having been spurned by these men all his life, Johnson could not resist embracing them—after first self-righteously scolding them. Once he had embraced them, he found himself committed to defending their policies, even when he disagreed with them. The southern leaders, of course, ate humble pie; it was a small enough price to pay to get what they wanted.

The restored governments themselves, contrary to the amnesty terms, acquired a decidedly Confederate tinge. Benjamin G. Humphries, the new governor of Mississippi, was a former Confederate general; the governor of South Carolina, James L. Orr, had been a Confederate senator; one of the U. S. senators-elect from Georgia, Alexander H. Stephens, was the former Vice-President of the Confederacy. Right down the line, according to a Louisiana Unionist, the public offices were being distributed "to men who held commissions in the rebel army, who signed the ordinance of secession. . . . You can see them now," he noted, "as judges, sheriffs and important officers of the new state."

Nor were these men "reconstructed" in any sense of the word. Governor Humphries in his inaugural address assured his constituents that "ours is and it shall ever be a government of white men." His sentiments were echoed by Governor Orr. The Democratic convention in Louisiana resolved that "the people of African descent cannot be considered as citizens of the United States." And John B. Baldwin of Virginia, anticipating the main line of white resistance to black equality, said of the blacks:

"I do not believe that, as a race, they will ever have the persistence of purpose, or the energy, or the intellectual vigor to rise to anything like intellectual equality with the white race. I think that they will get along very well in the ordinary domestic relations, as servants and inferiors."

Northern reaction to all this was predictable. "You enfranchise your enemies and disenfranchise your friends," Douglass told Johnson. *The Chicago Tribune* warned Mississippi that the North would convert the state into a frog pond before allowing the reestablishment of slavery. Stevens wrote to Johnson: "Among all the leading Union men of the North with whom I had intercourse I do not find one who approves of your policy. . . . Can you not hold your hand and wait the action of Congress? . . ." His letter, like a similar one that had preceded it, was not even acknowledged. "Is there no way," Stevens asked Sumner in desperation, "to arrest the insane course of the President in reconstruction?" Two days before Congress convened, Sumner had a long private interview with Johnson. Finding the President deeply "changed" and "unreasonable," Sumner left the White House convinced that "rebellion had vaulted into the presidential chair."

The 39th Congress was scheduled to convene on Monday, December 4, 1865. At a party caucus two days before, the radicals persuaded the moderates to join them in denying the newly elected southern senators and congressmen their seats on Monday, an idea originally proposed by Wendell Phillips.

Such an idea, the radicals' leader, Stevens, knew, would appeal to the party instincts of every Republican. Republicans outnumbered Democrats by 28 in the Senate and by 98 in the House. Seating the southerners, almost all of whom were Democrats, would shrink these majorities to about 6 in the Senate and about 40 in the House. No Republican fancied that. On the contrary, party strategists hoped through black suffrage to replace southern Democrats with reconstruction Republicans and consolidate Republican political power. Lincoln, aiming at the same end, if by different means, would have appreciated that; but Johnson, a Democrat, could hardly allow it.

Stevens' plan was to exclude the southerners by omitting their names from the roll call of the Congress. Johnson chose Congressman-elect Horace Maynard of Tennessee, a proven Unionist, to challenge the exclusion.

Monday at noon the House was called to order. The Clerk of the House began intoning the roll in alphabetical order. When he called, "William Niblick of Indiana," Maynard protested his omission and brandished his certification of election. Without rising, Stevens said, "I call the gentleman to order." The Clerk, a devoted admirer of Stevens, calmly announced: "The Clerk rules, as a matter of order, that he cannot recognize any gentleman whose name is not upon this roll." A motion to accept the completed roll was carried easily by the Republicans; the Senate followed suit. In one brilliant stroke Stevens had nullified Johnson's entire restoration program.

At Stevens' suggestion, the Republicans also voted to create a Joint Committee on Reconstruction to investigate conditions in the South and to consider all matters pertinent to reconstruction, including the qualifications of the excluded southern representatives. The Committee was composed of nine congressmen and six senators; twelve of the total were Republicans. Of these, at least half were radicals, including Stevens; the chairman, however, was a moderate, Senator William Pitt Fessenden of Maine.

At this point the dispute between Johnson and the radicals still was negotiable, because the moderates, who held the balance of power, were not committed to any reconstruction program. "I am ready and disposed to support the Executive to the best of my ability," Fessenden declared shortly after the Committee was formed. But he made it clear that he expected Congress to participate in any policy-making.

In February, 1866, Congress passed a bill extending the life of the Freedmen's Bureau and expanding its powers to include jurisdiction over alleged civil rights violations. The Bureau had been created during the last month of the war to assist displaced blacks—and whites, who used it more—with emergency food, shelter and clothing. It also had been authorized to confiscate and redistribute southern land holdings. But when the head of the Bureau had attempted to exercise this power, Johnson had issued an executive directive placing most property beyond the Bureau's reach.

Johnson now vetoed the extension of the Bureau on the grounds that "a system for the support of indigent persons in the United States was never contemplated by the authors of the Constitution. . . ." And, since the southern states had been denied a voice in the consideration of the bill, he added, it constituted "taxation without representation."

The veto was narrowly sustained in the Senate. But it was a Pyrrhic victory, for it drove the moderates into the radical camp and sealed an alliance that then proceeded to legislate its own reconstruction.

In the next decade, Congress passed ten major laws and originated two amendments to the Constitution to protect the black man's political and civil rights. These statutes represent white Americans' most ambitious attempt to apply to black Americans the spirit of the nation's declaration that "all men are created equal" and "are endowed by their Creator with certain unalienable Rights."

The first of these laws, the Civil Rights Act of 1866, was enacted on March 13. It provided blacks with "full and equal benefit of all laws and proceedings for the security of person and property, as is enjoyed by white citizens. . . ." Johnson vetoed it, citing among his reasons that it operated "in favor of the colored and against the white race." Congress promptly overrode the veto on April 9. Three months later it passed a revised version of the Freedmen's Bureau bill over another presidential veto.

To reinforce the constitutionality of the Civil Rights Act, Congress proposed the Fourteenth Amendment, making blacks citizens. Johnson publicly denounced the amendment and urged the legislatures of the southern states not to ratify it. Ten of the eleven restored governments followed his advice, and ratification was delayed until 1868, when new "reconstructed" southern governments approved it.

Two years later the Fifteenth Amendment, guaranteeing the blacks' right to vote, was ratified after almost perishing in Congress. The House had phrased the amendment to forbid abridgement of voting rights because of "race, color, or previous condition of servitude." But the Senate, anticipating the states' discriminatory use of poll taxes and literacy tests, had substituted in its text the words "race, color, nativity, property, education or creed." The House refused to concur with the Senate version. Such an amendment, the House leadership pointed out, might not be ratified, since Connecticut and Massachusetts required a literacy test, Rhode Island had a property qualification for naturalized citizens, and the "nativity" provision would be attacked by anti-Chinese elements in California.

Congress was deadlocked. Then Wendell Phillips published an editorial chastising the Senate for being too radical. The House version of the amendment, he wrote, covered "all the ground that the people are ready to occupy." Urging the Senate to adopt it, Phillips concluded: "For the first time in our lives we beseech them to be a little more *politicians*—and a little less reformers." Within days the Senate accepted the House version.

"That article saved the amendment," Congressman George Boutwell of Massachusetts, leader of the House forces, later wrote to Phillips. "Its influence was immediate and potential. Men thought that if you, the extremest radical, could accept the House proposition they might safely do the same." So in one of those ironic twists of history, the nation's greatest egalitarian was responsible for the adoption of an amendment whose loopholes later enabled southern states to disfranchise their black citizens.

Johnson, however, challenged the Republican policies long before they got as far as the Fourteenth and Fifteenth Amendments. In the 1866 Congressional elections, the President took his case to the people in a nineteen-day, 2,000 mile, preelection "swing around the circle" by train —the first large-scale presidential whistle-stop campaign. He pleaded for understanding, reviled the radical leaders and exchanged insults with hecklers in the crowds.

The radicals gave as good as they got, calling Johnson a drunkard and a traitor and "waving the bloody shirt" of the Civil War to rekindle smoldering sectional antagonisms. Johnson, remarked one moderate Republican, "returned to the Capitol personally discredited and politically ruined."

When the votes were counted, the Republicans had won control of the legislature and of the governorship of every northern state and had gained more than two-thirds majorities in the House and Senate. Every radical was returned to Congress, and several new ones were added.

Not the least of the reasons for the Republicans' sweeping victory were brutal attacks on blacks in Memphis and New Orleans during the summer. In Memphis a white mob, swelled by policemen, in a three-day drunken rampage against the black community, killed 46 and wounded 80; one white was injured. In New Orleans a similar mob, with the tacit support of police authorities, killed 34 blacks and four white Unionists and injured 200. Reporting on

Patience on a Monument. Thomas Nast, in *Harper's Weekly*, October 10, 1868. The New York Public Library.

the New Orleans massacre, General Philip H. Sheridan said that "the killing was in a manner so unnecessary and atrocious as to compel me to say it was murder."

Secure in its power, the Republican Congress on March 2, 1867 passed the First Reconstruction Act. It divided the South into five military districts for the purposes of holding new elections and forming new governments under federal supervision. Under this Act, blacks were qualified to vote and to hold office, and former Confederate officials were barred from either. New state constitutions embodying these provisions also were required, and they had to be approved by popular vote and by Congress. Finally, each state had to ratify the Fourteenth Amendment. Once these requirements were fulfilled, a state became eligible for readmission to the Union.

Congress followed this legislation with three supplementary acts that closed off loopholes in the original law. All four acts were passed over presidential vetoes.

Stevens and Sumner argued to include a program of land reform in the First Reconstruction Act. "If the South is ever to be made a safe Republic," Stevens suggested, "let her lands be cultivated by the toil of the owners, or the free labor of intelligent citizens." Stevens wanted to redistribute 394 million acres of land belonging to 70,000 of the "chief rebels," giving 40 acres to every adult freedman and selling the rest, the proceeds to be applied to the public debt and to disabled veterans' pensions. But such a proposal, even though it involved appropriating the land of less than five percent of the white populace, was too revolutionary for the moderates and even for some of the radicals. They didn't understand that freedom without an economic base to support it is like a castle in sand—doomed to topple. Then, too, they saw land reform as an attack upon property rights, and there is nothing more sacrosanct in America. So land reform was put to rest; the middle class wouldn't live with it.

Indeed, land reform was not the only casualty of conventional white middle-class attitudes. The economic and educational assistance necessary to help blacks shed the degradations of two centuries of slavery never materialized because few nineteenth century Americans realized their importance. Self-reliance was everything. "Let all the natural laws of labor, wages, competition . . . come into play, and the sooner will habits of responsibility, industry, self-dependence and manliness be developed," wrote a northern educator in Port Royal, one of the sites of early land reform.

A few hard-core radicals like Stevens and Sumner argued for economic aid programs. But not enough moderates—or even radicals—were willing to join their ranks. Even the Freedmen's Bureau, the one modest federal attempt at social rehabilitation, was allowed to expire by Congress in 1869.

Tradition persists in portraying the radicals as a band of unscrupulous politicians who substituted for Johnson's conciliatory program a harsh, vindictive policy, which for generations poisoned race relations in the South. But close examination of the record reveals that the radicals sought 100 years ago what enlightened Americans seek today: protection of the black man's civil and political rights.

The hard-core radicals, whipped on by spite and political hubris, foolishly impeached Johnson in 1868, and narrowly missed convicting him. They would have done better to indict their constituents. Indeed, one of them, George W. Julian, did. "The real trouble," he told his fellow Indianans, "is that *we hate the Negro.* It is not his ignorance that offends us, but his color."

"It is a grand thing to have rights secured by constitutional provisions and by legal enactments, but without a public opinion and a government to enforce them, they are a mockery."

Frederick Douglass

RECONSTRUCTION IN BLACK AND WHITE

1. Although few whites understood or cared about the black man's predicament, their representatives in Congress—motivated by political, economic and humane considerations—opened the way for his participation in the political process. The result was reconstruction, a memorable decade during which the black man was exposed briefly to the benefits and hazards of representative democracy.

The First Reconstruction Act of 1867 required the former Confederate states to form new governments and draft new constitutions in which the black man would be able to vote and hold office. By August, 1870, each of the eleven southern states had done so.

Traditional historians have portrayed these reconstructed governments as "repressive" and "barbaric." Actually the constitutions upon which they were based were not unlike the ones they replaced except in the area of political and civil rights for blacks. "The equality of all persons before the law," stated the new constitution of Arkansas, "is recognized and shall ever remain inviolate; nor shall any citizen ever be deprived of any right, privilege, or immunity, nor exempted from any burden or duty, on account of race, color, or previous condition." Most of the new constitutions echoed these sentiments.

Segregation of the races, however—especially in schools—remained the social norm. The issue being too explosive, most governments evaded it. Only two states, Louisiana and South Carolina, dealt with it constitutionally. They provided for integrated school systems; but, as might be expected, the enforcement of the law left much to be desired.

Blacks themselves were active in the drafting of most of these constitutions. The ratio of black delegates in the constitutional conventions ranged from 10 percent in Texas to 61 percent in South Carolina. Indeed, perhaps the truest measure of black reconstruction is reflected in the constitution of South Carolina, the only state in which the blacks were in the majority in the constitutional convention.

In the opinion of its detractors, the state's new constitution was "the work of sixty odd Negroes, many of them ignorant and depraved, together with fifty white men, outcasts of northern society, and southern renegades, betrayers of their race and country." If so, they did a good job. Not only did the constitution give the vote and free public education to everyone, it also abolished debt imprisonment, reduced taxes of the poor, extended women's rights and reformed the courts, the county governments and the electoral process.

The South Carolina convention, noted black Congressman Joseph Rainey, "adopted a liberal constitution, securing alike equal rights to all citizens, white and black, male and female, as far as possible. Mark you, we did not discriminate, although we had a majority." A white man, Woodrow Wilson's Assistant Secretary of Labor, who had lived under this document, said of it: "By every truly democratic test, that Negro-made constitution of South Carolina stands shoulder high above the white man's constitution that it superseded."

In the long run, of course, a constitution is just a scrap of paper; it is men who govern. The men governing the reconstructed states fell into four general groups. Most powerful were those northerners who had recently come South, so-called "carpetbaggers." Cooperating with them were so-called "scalawags," southerners who were loyal to the Union. Both of these groups were dependent upon the votes of the third group, the blacks. The fourth group, southern conservatives, unreconstructed Democrats for the most part, were a powerful minority who eventually "redeemed" each state.

None of these groups fits the conventional historian's stereotype of it. There were honest as well as dishonest carpetbaggers, distinguished as well as disreputable scalawags, responsible as well as irresponsible blacks, respectable as well as fanatical conservatives.

The most enduring caricatures have been those of the carpetbaggers. One historian describes them as "too depraved, dissolute, dishonest and degraded to get the lowest of places in the states they had just left," and the history books reflect that assessment in varying degrees.

Some carpetbaggers *were* unscrupulous adventurers. But many more were ordinary school teachers, veterans, merchants and federal clerks seeking a better life in a new South. As a group they were no better nor worse than most Americans. Although many of them were radicals politically, their attitudes toward blacks were still colored by the racism that pervaded American society, North and South. B.H. True, a New Yorker living in Georgia, spoke for most whites when he said he was friendly to blacks, "but there is an antagonism which we all have against the race; that I cannot get rid of; I do not believe any man can."

Scalawags usually are written off as poor, mean whites. The term itself probably is derived from the name of a district in the Shetland Islands, Scalloway, where runty cattle and horses called "Shetland ponies" are bred. A contemporary description of scalawags as "scaly, scabby runts in a herd of cattle" seems to bear this out. Like carpetbaggers, however, scalawags have been unfairly portrayed. Some were corrupt, others were opportunists; but most were moderate southerners who for their own reasons had opposed secession. This is not to say they were pro-black. Far from it. Most of them opposed black equality. Indeed, some southerners became scalawags because, as James L. Orr of South Carolina explained, it was "important for our prominent men to identify themselves with the radicals for the purpose of controlling their action and preventing mischief to the state."

"Mischief" is what most white people expected from the blacks in their new role as citizens, voters and, in some cases, legislators. Indeed, the stereotype of the black man as shiftless and irresponsible persists even today. But evidence indicates that the blacks acted as any large group does—some nobly, some badly and most indifferently. Describing the blacks in the South Carolina legislature, historians Francis B. Simkins and Robert H. Woody wrote: "There was a large proportion of former slaves, and at first perhaps two-thirds of them could not write, but by 1871 most of them had learned at least to read and write. Many of them were speakers of force and eloquence, while others were silent or crude."

The first black Senator and Representatives—looking as white as possible. The Library of Congress.

In the eyes of the fourth group, the southern conservatives, the three other groups were anathema. During reconstruction the public debt in the southern states increased astronomically, and taxes rose correspondingly. Some of the money was siphoned off by corrupt officials and fraudulent businessmen. The conservatives blamed the carpetbaggers, scalawags and blacks and the radical governments they administered. But as historian W.E.B. Du

Bois noted of the situation in South Carolina: "There was after the war a severe economic strain upon the former wealthy ruling class, and if South Carolina had been ruled by angels during 1868–1876 the protest of wealth and property would have been shrill and angry, and it would have had all the justification that the war-ridden always have."

Actually, the taxes were not all that high. The rate of taxation in South Carolina from 1868–1872 was nine mills on the dollar; from 1872–1876 it rose to just over eleven mills. In Mississippi the rate rose from one mill in 1869 to fourteen mills in 1874. But compared to such northern states as New York, Pennsylvania and Illinois, where the average rate was more than 21 mills, these rates still were low.

In any case, the increase in taxation and debt was not without reason. The radical governments rebuilt the public facilities of their states and vastly increased social services. In South Carolina, for example, only one-eighth of the *white* children of school age were enrolled in school when the radicals assumed power. The number amounted to 30,000. By 1876, 123,000 children, black and white, were in school.

"We were eight years in power," said one black legislator. "We . . . built schoolhouses, established charitable institutions, built and maintained the penitentiary system, provided for the education of the deaf and dumb, rebuilt the jails and courthouses, rebuilt the bridges and reestablished the ferries. In short, we . . . reconstructed the state and placed it upon the road to prosperity. . . ." Somebody had to pay for all this.

The source of much of the graft was also the cause of much of the public debt: railroad construction. And in the matter of rigging railroad contracts no group held a monopoly. A contemporary Georgia editor noted that the extravagance and corruption of the times "benefitted about as many Democrats as Republicans." And E. Merton Coulter, an antiradical historian, admitted that a Democratic administration in Alabama "in lack of honesty differed little from the administrations of the radicals between whom it was sandwiched."

But corruption was not the real issue; equality was. The radical governments, despite what one historian called "the incompetence of some, the dishonesty of a few, and above all the inexperience of most of the officeholders," almost wrought a social revolution in the South. What brought them up short in the end was the absence of land reform, indomitable racism, southern intransigence and northern indifference.

The southern conservatives' counterrevolution began in violence and ended in fraud. In the absence of radical reconciliation and land reform, such a progression was predictable. South Carolina Democrats warned blacks in 1868 that their power could not endure, whether they used it for good or ill. They proved correct. In 1870 Tennessee, North Carolina and Virginia (even as it was being readmitted into the Union) were "redeemed" by the Democrats. Texas followed in 1873, Alabama and Arkansas the next year and Mississippi in 1875. By 1876 only the *idea* of reconstruction remained to be destroyed; reconstruction itself already had fallen in all but three southern states.

The violence began early. In 1866 radical journalist Carl Schurz wrote of his postwar tour of the South: "Some planters held back their former slaves on their plantations by brute force. Armed bands of white men patrolled the county roads to drive back the Negroes wandering about. Dead bodies of murdered Negroes were found on and near the highways and byways." Describing the situation in Alabama, Mississippi and Louisiana, Schurz wrote: "The life of a Negro is not worth much there. I have seen one who was shot in the leg while he was riding a mule, because the ruffian thought it more trouble to ask him to get off the mule than to shoot him."

Random violence soon was succeeded by organized terrorism. The Ku Klux Klan was formed in Tennessee in 1866, and its network of secret "dens" rapidly spread to form the "Invisible Empire of the South." Wearing white hoods and robes, Klansmen rode the land at night, intimidating, beating or murdering "undesirable" blacks and whites—all in the name of chivalry, humanity, mercy and patriotism. If blacks, said one freedman, "got so they made good money and had a good farm, the Ku Klux would come and murder 'em. The government builded schoolhouses, and the Ku Klux went to work and burned 'em down. They'd go to the jails and take the colored men out and knock their brains out and break their necks and throw 'em in the river." Members of such radical organizations as the Union League, which instructed blacks in their voting rights, also became special targets of Klan violence.

Other white supremacy "societies" arose all over the South, many of them with grand sounding names like the Knights of the White Camelia, the White Brotherhood and the White League. Together with the Klan, they conducted a reign of terror. A congressional committee investigating the Klan's activities in nine South Carolina counties in 1871 recorded a total for six months of 35 men lynched, 262 men and women whipped, and 101 more shot, mutilated or burned out of their homes. During the same period, blacks in these counties killed four, beat one and committed 16 "outrages." In Louisiana 2,000 blacks and Republican leaders were killed or wounded within the few weeks before the 1868 presidential election. As a result of the terrorism, one election district, with a registered Republican majority of 1,071 voters, did not cast a *single* ballot for Grant; all 4,787 votes went to the Democrats.

Some blacks were for meeting violence with violence. "Give us guns," one militant begged the Republican governor of Mississippi, "and we will show the scoundrels that colored people *will fight*." But few blacks could get weapons, and those who could often had them taken away by local sheriffs. Besides, most blacks still trusted the government. Warning the militants against action, a Georgia preacher reminded them that "this would not do; that the whole South would then come against us and kill us off, as the Indians have been killed off. Better," the preacher cautioned his flock, "to apply to the government for protection. . . ."

The reconstructed state governments tried to provide some protection. Tennessee in 1868 passed legislation declaring Klanlike activities punishable by jail and fines, and within two years most other southern states had done the same. Congress also acted in 1870 and 1871, passing three "enforcement" laws to protect blacks against intimidation, especially at the polls, by persons who "band or conspire together, or go in disguise upon the public highway." The third law, the so-called Ku Klux Act (April 20, 1871), declared that the activities of "unlawful combinations" constituted a rebellion against the government of the United States." It imposed penalties of up to $5,000 or six years in prison for those who deprived "any person or any class of persons of the equal protection of the laws, or of equal privileges or immunities under the laws."

These laws, however, were for the most part ineffective. The Klan simply went underground and claimed it didn't exist. Those alleged offenders who were arrested were seldom convicted; witnesses were reluctant to testify, white juries were even more reluctant to convict. The law is only as effective as the apparatus for its enforcement is just, and the apparatus was still white. As one traditional historian admits: "Race prejudice thus checked the rigid application of the law."

To violence, the conservatives added deception. They began blaming the corruption and mismanagement of the reconstruction governments on the blacks, a myth that persists even today. It was brilliant strategy. No one approves of corruption. And white northerners who might deplore the violence of the Klan could be convinced of blacks' alleged greed and incompetence, because such accusations confirmed their basic feeling that blacks were *inferior*.

The public was getting tired of the blacks' problems, anyway. By 1872 the northern businessman was demanding "law and order" to protect his investment. To get it, he was willing to look the other way in the matter of the black man's rights. In 1874 the country dropped into the most drastic depression in its history up to that time; it lasted four years, causing thousands of business failures and severe unemployment. That same year the Democrats won a majority in the House, and Grant refused a request from Mississippi's radical governor, Adelbert Ames, for federal troops. The great majority of the public, Grant explained, "are ready now to condemn any interference on the part of the government."

The radical leaders also were fewer in number. Thaddeus Stevens had died in 1868. The next year Benjamin F. Wade lost his seat in the Senate, and in 1870 George W. Julian lost his in the House. Charles Sumner, the staunchest of the radicals, died in 1874. Since 1867 he had been trying to get a comprehensive civil rights bill through Congress, and he continued his efforts to the end. As he lay on his deathbed, surrounded by friends and officials, Sumner three times cried out: "You must take care of the civil rights bill—my bill, the civil rights bill—don't let it fail!" It was his last testament.

The following year a civil rights bill omitting Sumner's provision for integrated public schools was passed by Congress. Known as the Civil Rights Act of 1875, it made an "appropriate object of legislation" the social segregation imposed upon blacks in most states—northern as well as southern. All persons, declared the act, "shall be entitled to the full and equal enjoyment of the accommodations, advantages, facilities, and privileges of inns, public conveyances on land or water, theaters and other places of public amusement." It also prohibited the exclusion of anyone from jury service on racial grounds.

The Civil Rights Act was declared unconstitutional by the Supreme Court in 1883. Actually, the increasing indifference of white America to the black man's plight had made the law a dead letter even as it was passed. As Frederick Douglass observed: "It is a grand thing to have rights secured by constitutional provisions and legal enactments, but without a public opinion and a government to enforce them, they are a mockery."

Reconstruction had entered a terminal stage. "What the South now needs," said a leading Republican businessman in 1875, "is capital to develop her resources, but this she cannot obtain . . . while things remain as they are." It had been a mistake, the businessman added, to lead the southern blacks to believe "that the United States government was their friend, rather than those with whom their lot is cast, among whom they must live and for whom they must work. We have tried this long enough. Now let the South alone."

Southern moderates, sensing which way the wind was

blowing, deserted the Republican party in droves. Said one prominent Mississippi scalawag: "No white man can live in the South in the future and act with any other than the Democratic party unless he is willing and prepared to live a life of social isolation and remain in political oblivion . . . I must yield to the inevitable and surrender my convictions upon the altar of my family's good."

Not content with these developments, Mississippi Democrats formed armed militia groups and terrorized black voters in the state elections of 1875. "We are in the hands of murderers," stated a letter signed by 300 Vicksburg voters. "They say they will carry this election either by ballot or bullet." When Governor Ames again asked for federal troops, Ohio Republicans warned Grant that if he sent troops to Mississippi, the party would lose Ohio, where an election also was in progress. Grant decided to sacrifice the Mississippi blacks on the altar of Ohio. His Attorney General replied to Ames that the people were "tired of these annual autumnal outbreaks in the South." Ames took this as final proof that the executive branch of the government "had decided that the reconstruction acts of Congress were a failure."

The Supreme Court, which usually reflects popular political sentiment, now pulled the legal props from under reconstruction. For some years the Court had avoided ruling on reconstruction issues. But between 1870 and 1874 Grant made four appointments to the Court that changed its complexion. In 1873 the Court, in the so-called "Slaughterhouse" case, ruled by a vote of five to four that there was a difference between *national* and *state* citizenship and that there were no constitutional guarantees against violation of state citizenship. Frederick Douglass correctly saw that for the blacks "dual citizenship means no citizenship."

Three years later the Court went one step further, undercutting the Fourteenth Amendment and the "enforcement" act of 1870. The case, *United States* v. *Cruikshank,* involved three white Louisianans who had been part of a mob that broke up a peaceful political meeting of blacks, killing two of them. Morrison R. Waite, the new Chief Justice, delivered the Court's opinion. Where the Fourteenth Amendment guaranteed the rights of citizens, he explained, it did so against infringement by the *states* but not against action by private *individuals.* And since the blacks' meeting had been convened to discuss *local* politics, the enforcement act could not apply because it covered only acts connected with *national* citizenship. So much for white justice.

The final blow to reconstruction was delivered in the presidential election of 1876. Rutherford B. Hayes, governor of Ohio and a former Union general, a moderate with "sound"—that is, probusiness—economic views, was the Republican candidate. His opponent was Governor Samuel J. Tilden of New York, a former corporation lawyer, a man who also had the proper business instincts. Tilden, a reform governor, made "Grantism" and corruption in the so-called "black–carpetbagger" governments the main campaign issue. The Republicans, vulnerable on the issue of corruption and saddled with a two-year-old depression, conjured up the old war devils. "Soldiers," exhorted one Republican, "every scar you have got on your heroic bodies was given you by a Democrat."

The result was perhaps the most shameful election in American history. Although Tilden won in the count of the popular vote, he fell one short of the 185 votes needed for victory in the Electoral College. He had carried New York, New Jersey, Connecticut, Indiana and, of course, all the "redeemed" southern states. Hayes had won 166 electoral votes, carrying most of the Northeast and Midwest and all of the Far West. In Florida, South Carolina and Louisiana—the three remaining southern states under Republican control—the election returns were disputed.

The Democrats had muscled their way to victory in these three states. As one conservative South Carolinian admitted: "By a system of violence and coercion, ranging through all possible grades, from urgent persuasion to mob violence, the election was won by Democrats." But the Republicans, who controlled the election machinery in each state, rejected the fraudulent returns and certified Republican electors. Each party accused the other of fraud and refused to budge.

Tilden needed one of these states for victory, Hayes needed all three. The House, controlled by the Democrats, and the Senate, controlled by the Republicans, dispatched separate committees to investigate the election returns. Each found what it sought. Finally, a bipartisan electoral committee of five House members, five Senate members and five Supreme Court justices was created to settle the issue. They voted eight to seven, along strict party lines, to certify the Republican electors, and on March 4, Hayes was declared President by an electoral vote of 185 to 184. But this was only the tip of the iceberg, the part that showed above water; the bulk of the negotiations had been carried on below the water line.

It is popularly assumed that the Democrats agreed to Hayes' election in return for the withdrawal of federal troops from the South and the promise of no federal interference in state affairs. These were the conditions agreed upon by advisors and representatives of Hayes and Tilden in a series of conferences on February 26th at the Wormley House, an exclusive Washington Hotel. (James Wormley, the owner, was black—a nice touch.) But these concessions by Republicans would not by themselves have moved the Democrats. Only a few troops remained in South Carolina and Louisiana, anyway, and Tilden already was committed to remove them. So the Democrats could have held out for home rule *and* the presidency. There had to be something more, and there was: money.

The South had been hit even harder than the North by the long depression; it desperately needed economic assistance. Aid was something the federal government could provide, especially in the form of railway subsidies, but only with Republican assent. The Republicans offered to support these subsidies as part of a presidential "arrangement." The Democrats agreed to the exchange, Hayes for subsidies. Reconstruction ended. The troops went home; the government looked the other way; the public went about its business. A curtain of indifference dropped over the nation. The black man was again alone.

"The white folks had all the courts, all the guns, all the hounds, all the railroads . . . all the newspapers, all the money, and nearly all the land—and we had only our ignorance, our poverty and our empty hands."

Survivor of a Georgia forced-labor camp

THE JIM CROW ERA

"Hayes has sold us all out," complained one prominent Republican shortly after the accommodation of 1877.

The President, of course, didn't like to think of it that way. "I considered the situation of things in the South . . . " he told a reporter at the beginning of a southern goodwill tour in September, 1877, "and I asked myself why is it, and how long must this continue." In a dozen speeches along the tour route he framed his answer.

In Louisville, addressing a large crowd waving Confederate banners and shouting the rebel yell, he talked about "a vast Confederacy" that would be "a refuge for every race and every clime to come together." His words were followed by heavy applause, but a reporter noted that the blacks in the crowd were "less enthusiastic." In Chattanooga, Hayes assured his "colored friends" that "with the bayonets removed from the South, the people of all colors would be safer in every light, in every interest, than they ever were when protected merely by the bayonet." And in Atlanta he told the blacks in the crowd; "I believe that your rights and interests would be safer if this great mass of intelligent white men"—he looked around him—"were let alone by the general government." Prolonged cheers. But whether or not the blacks joined in them was not recorded.

After the tour, Hayes summed up his impressions. "I believe," he told a reporter, "the era of good feeling between the North and the South is permanent."

The "good feeling" that Hayes perceived was mostly between white men. The little that spilled across racial lines was not enough to dilute the racism that washed over the entire society. Basic attitudes had not changed much. A falling-out among white men had given the black man his freedom and a measure of civil rights; now the reconciliation of whites paved the way for the reduction of that freedom and the suppression of those rights.

It happened gradually, and at a different pace in the different states. For example, the first law disfranchising blacks was not passed until 1890 in Mississippi, and the last was not passed until 1910 in Oklahoma. Although it long had been the practice to segregate blacks from whites on trains in the South (and often in the North), most southern states did not adopt the "Jim Crow" * laws that made it mandatory until the 1890's. As late as 1885 a black newspaperman traveling from Boston to South Carolina with "a chip on [his] shoulder" could report: "I feel about as safe here as in Providence, R.I. I can ride in first-class cars on the railroads and in the streets. I can . . . drink a glass of soda and be more politely waited upon than in some parts of New England."

On the old plantations, however, it wasn't so rosy. Never

---

* In 1830 entertainer Thomas Rice created a blackface song and dance routine modeled after the sidewalk performance of a black minstrel. Part of the refrain was: "Wheel about, turn about, dance jest so/ Every time I wheel about I shout Jim Crow!"

good, the condition of the mass of black agricultural workers quickly deteriorated after the accommodation. Intimidation deprived them of the ballot, and the tenant farming system locked them into virtual slavery. Under this system poor blacks (and poor whites) rented the land they tilled and, until their crop was harvested, bought their provisions on credit against the value of the expected harvest. Interest rates were so high, however, that the tenant farmer seldom cleared his debts, which were carried over and added to new ones. After a while the overburdened farmer was a slave to the plantation owner's ledger book. If he got out of line, what little he might own—a mule or a plow—could be confiscated by the landowner to "pay off" the debt.

Left without hope or dignity, black agricultural workers began to leave the South. Migration committees and secret societies sprang up to organize a mass exodus of blacks. By 1879 one Louisiana committee had on its rolls almost 93,000 men and women from Louisiana, Mississippi, Texas and Arkansas. That same year 50,000 blacks, most of them from Louisiana's cotton belt, left their homes. "There was no hope for us and we had better go," one organizer told a Senate investigating committee. "The largest majority of the people, of the white people, that held us as slaves treats our people so bad in many respects that it is impossible for them to stand it."

Dressed in rags, dragging their few possessions in boxes and bundles, black workers and their families crowded onto Mississippi steamboats headed upriver. In Kansas a Freedman's Relief Association provided temporary shelter and food for the migrants. Those who could find work settled in the state, the others drifted further north up to Chicago or west to the territories. They were not always welcomed. In Lincoln, Nebraska, 150 migrants were driven out of town, and in Denver, Colorado, white landlords refused to rent to them. But few "exodusters" returned south.

Poor blacks continued to stream out of the South until the end of the century. Most, however, remained, and they were subjected to increasing oppression. They became the victims of the southern whites' political, economic and social frustrations. Historian C. Vann Woodward, however, notes that the increased oppression of the blacks was less the result of intensified racism than of the relaxation of the opposition to it. "All the elements of fear, jealousy, proscription, hatred, and fanaticism had long been present, as they are present in various degrees of intensity in any society," he explains. "What enabled them to rise to dominance was . . . a general weakening and discrediting of the numerous forces that had hitherto kept them in check."

One of these restraining forces was the law of the land. Since 1873 the Supreme Court had been undermining civil rights legislation. In 1877, in *Hall* v. *de Cuir,* it overturned a Louisiana law of 1869 that prohibited racial segregation on public carriers. "If the public good requires such legislation," the Court declared, "it must come from Congress and not from the states." Then in 1883, in ruling on just such a federal law, the Court struck it down. It was an historic decision.

Five suits, the so-called "Civil Rights" cases, had been brought against individuals and corporations for denying blacks accommodations in hotels, theaters and on a train. The complaints were based upon the Civil Rights Act of 1875. By a vote of eight to one, the Court ruled that the basic "accommodations" section of the 1875 law was not supported by either the Thirteenth or the Fourteenth Amendment. The Thirteenth Amendment prohibited slavery; but racial discrimination, the Court explained, was not a "badge of slavery." And the Fourteenth Amendment did not cover "individual invasions of individual rights."

John Marshall Harlan, the dissenting justice, thought these grounds "entirely too narrow and artificial. I cannot resist the conclusion," the Kentucky Unionist stated, "that the substance and spirit of the recent amendments of the Constitution have been sacrificed by a subtle and ingenious verbal criticism."

In 1890 Mississippi passed a law *requiring* segregation on public carriers, and the Court, in another show of subtle ingenuity, upheld it. That same year Louisiana passed a similar law requiring "equal but separate accommodations for the white and colored races" on passenger trains. Homer Adolphe Plessy, a light-skinned black, challenged the law by refusing to ride in the "colored" coach of a train, and his case, *Plessy* v. *Ferguson,* reached the Supreme Court in 1896. Plessy's lawyer, Albion W. Tourgee, based his arguments on the Thirteenth and Fourteenth Amendments, adding: "Justice is pictured blind and her daughter, the Law, ought at least to be color blind." The Court, however, decided against Plessy. Repeating some previous interpretations, it added a new one: that the Fourteenth Amendment could enforce political equality but not social equality or "a commingling of the two races upon terms unsatisfactory to either." Declaring that legislation is powerless to eradicate "racial instincts," the Court concluded: "If one race be inferior to the other socially, the Constitution of the United States cannot put them upon the same plane."

Justice Harlan, dissenting again, predicted that the Court's ruling eventually would prove to be "quite as pernicious" as that made in the *Dred Scott* case, which in 1857 had established the principle that a black man was not a citizen and had no rights. History proved him correct. For 58 years *Plessy* v. *Ferguson* was cited as the legal justification for racial segregation based upon the principle of "separate but equal" facilities. The blacks themselves for decades accepted the principle of separation and sought merely equal facilities—without much success.

All this, it should be noted, was decreed by a Supreme Court dominated not by southerners but by northerners. The 1883 Court contained only two southerners (both Republicans); the 1896 Court, only one. That all except Harlan, however, should institutionalize racism is not surprising. Northern (and western) sentiment on racial segregation differed little from that of the South. Indeed, as Professor Woodward points out in his history, *The Strange Career of Jim Crow,* systematized segregation "was born in the North and reached an advanced age before moving South in force."

Despite the fact that slavery was virtually abolished in the North by 1830, the northern black never was allowed to forget that he was "inferior" and socially "undesirable." He was segregated on trains, in theaters, restaurants and hotels, in schools, in churches and hospitals, even in prisons and cemeteries. "In virtually every phase of existence," says historian Leon F. Litvack in his book *North of Slavery,* "Negroes found themselves systematically separated from whites."

In the North as well as in the South, job opportunities were closed to blacks. So were the unions. As a result, complained one black leader, his people were "compelled to loiter around the edges of industry." In northern cities, blacks were early crowded into ghettos. This didn't happen in southern cities until well after the Civil War. Even then, one black who had lived on both sides of the Mason–Dixon line said: "I think the whites of the South are really less afraid to [have] contact with colored people than the whites of the North."

It is true that fifteen northern states passed civil rights

legislation after the Supreme Court struck down the federal Civil Rights Act in 1883. But in practice these laws were ineffectual, and the pattern of segregation remained unchanged. Indeed, one observer noted that "throughout the North there was not only acquiescence among the white population in the 'Southern Way' of solving the race problem, but a tendency to imitate it in practice." By 1896 *The New York Times* could report the crucial Plessy ruling under "railroad news," a sure sign of its readers' real sentiments.

The principal victim of prejudice in the North at the turn of the century was the newly arrived immigrant. Only 2 percent of the northern population was black. But these few were set apart by *race*, not national origin, a prejudice which is more virulent—and more enduring. "The Negro is an ape," declared *The Negro Is a Beast,* a widely circulated book in 1900, and no act, "whether legislative, executive or judicial," could change his status in the universe.

In the more sophisticated, supposedly enlightened journals, such as *Harper's*, *Atlantic* and *Scribner's,* respectable sociologists and biologists twisted Charles Darwin's theory on evolution to prove that blacks were inferior. And not only blacks but Indians and Chinese as well. The idea of "Manifest Destiny" was in the air, and inferior races had to be put in their place. Theodore Roosevelt in 1895 observed: "A perfectly stupid race can never rise to a very high plane; the Negro, for instance, has been kept down as much by lack of intellectual development as anything else."

Black women fared no better than black men. In 1900 the General Federation of Women's Clubs became involved in a controversy over the exclusion of a black women's club. The Chicago *Transcript*, amused, asked: "Why cannot the clubwomen do as the men do at their clubs, and tacitly agree to give soul-stirring, hair-raising questions the go-by?" The genteel president of the Federation blamed it all on the light-skinned black woman who had forced the issue: "It is the 'high-caste' Negroes who bring about all the ill-feeling. The ordinary colored woman understands her position thoroughly." That position was as a domestic.

In the press, in books, on the stage, in cartoons—blacks were portrayed as lazy, stupid, irresponsible, deceitful, immoral, improvident chicken thieves. One historical and literary critic lists seven stereotypes of blacks: Contented Slave, Wretched Freedman, Comic Negro, Brute Negro, Tragic Mulatto, Local Color Negro, and Exotic Primitive. Joel Chandler Harris' beloved Uncle Remus could, and did, say: "What's a nigger gwineter 'larn outen books? I kin take a bar'l stave an' fling mo' sense inter a nigger in one minnit dan all de schoolhouses betwixt dis en de state er Midgigin." And in Mark Twain's *Huckleberry Finn* (1884), one of the few novels in which blacks are not stereotyped, the following exchange occurs between Huck and Aunt Sally after a steamboat accident:

"Good gracious! Anybody hurt?"
"No'm. Killed a nigger."
"Well, it's lucky because sometimes people do get hurt."

That says it all about the status of blacks, North and South, East and West.

It was this atmosphere that preserved traditional *de facto* segregation in the North and imposed mandatory *legal* segregation in the South. "God Almighty drew the color line and it cannot be obliterated," said the Richmond *Times* in 1900, and the paper demanded rigid segregation "in every relation of southern life." One by one, the southern states legislated segregation on trolleys and steamboats, in waiting rooms and amusement parks, in residential neighborhoods. "White Only" signs appeared on drinking fountains, toilets, entrances and exits. The schools had remained segregated all through reconstruction; now Florida law required that the textbooks used by black and white children be kept separate even in storage!

Southern blacks also lost the ballot. For some years they had been disfranchised systematically by force and fraud. Then in 1890 Mississippi adopted a new constitution to do it legally. Under the "Mississippi plan," all voters had to be able to read and to understand any clause in the state constitution. How well they read was determined by local election officials—who, of course, were white. Variations of this "understanding clause" were adopted by South Carolina in 1895, Louisiana in 1898, North Carolina in 1900, Alabama in 1901, Virginia in 1902, Georgia in 1908, and Oklahoma in 1910. The Supreme Court upheld the Mississippi law in 1898.

To the "understanding clause" were added property qualifications, the poll tax and the "white primary." In most southern states, winning the Democratic nomination in the party primary was tantamount to winning the election because the Republicans were so weak. Blacks were excluded from the primary elections by limiting party membership to whites. "The Negro as a political force," observed a southern spokesman around the turn of the century, "has dropped out of serious consideration."

What was left for the black man? Very little. "The white folks had all the courts, all the guns, all the hounds, all the railroads . . . all the newspapers, all the money, and nearly all the land—and we had only our ignorance, our poverty and our empty hands," protested a survivor of a Georgia forced-labor camp. This man had spent 30 years in peonage, a slave in all but name. As President William McKinley intoned at his inaugural in 1896 that "these years of glorious history have exalted mankind and advanced the cause of freedom throughout the world," this black man—and thousands like him—was living in what he described as "hell itself."

In 1905, when he was over 40 years old, he told his story. As a boy of ten he had been bound out by his uncle to a white plantation owner, who had put him to work in the fields from sunrise to sundown, in all weather, six days a week. Deliberately kept uneducated, he had been, in his own words, "a man nearly grown before I knew how to count from one to one hundred."

At 21, his apprenticeship completed, he had been persuaded by the owner to make a one-year contract to work for $3.50 a week and the use of a one-room log cabin. Soon after, he had married a house servant and, with a gift from the owner of $25 worth of furniture, they had moved into a two-room shanty.

For five years he renewed his contract; then the owner died and his son, a state senator, suggested that the man sign a ten-year contract so he "wouldn't have to fix up papers every year." He made his mark. Shortly afterwards, the Senator brought in 40 convict laborers—black, of course—he had leased from the state at $200 a year each, a common practice. Shackled and guarded, the convicts were stabled like horses in a long, low shanty with crude double-decker bunks in each stall. The free laborers wanted to quit, the man recalled, but the Senator sent word that he would "hold us to the letter of the contract, or put us in chains and lock us up—the same as the other prisoners." A virtual prisoner, he worked out his contract, toiling in the fields side by side with the convicts, eating the same slop, only sleeping separately.

When their contracts expired, the free laborers refused to renew them. The Senator accepted that and wished them well. Before they left, however, he said they must sign an acknowledgment of the "debts" they had incurred at his commissary, where they had been required to buy their food and clothing. The amounts "owed" were arbitrary, "but no one of us would have dared to dispute a white man's word," the laborer explained. They made their marks.

That night they were rounded up by the sheriff and locked up in the stalls with the convicts. The paper they had signed not only acknowledged their alleged debt but also required them to work it off for the Senator. "And from that day forward we were treated like convicts. Really, we had made ourselves lifetime slaves, or peons, as the laws called us."

Soon afterwards his nine-year-old son was "given away," never to be seen again, and his wife was taken as a mistress by one of the white guards. The man could not even protest: "It would have meant death on the spot to have said a word." After working three years to clear his alleged $165 debt, he was given a new pair of overalls, taken across the state line, and told to "git." He did.

His was not an isolated case; indeed, if there was anything unusual about it, it was the fact that he survived. A southern white woman wrote that "the cruel treatment of the helpless human chattel in the hands of guards is such as no tongue can tell nor pen picture." And George W. Cable, a southern writer, estimated that the death rate in the Louisiana convict camps, judging from the rates in the other southern states, "must exceed that of any pestilence that ever fell upon Europe in the Middle Ages."

Every southern state had its convict farms where poor blacks (and some poor whites) were sent by the courts to "work off" petty fines. In some cases the charges were technical, in others they were trumped up; even when the

Benediction in Georgia. Lithograph by George Wesley Bellows. The Cleveland Museum of Art. Gift of Leonard C. Hanna, Jr.

charge was legitimate, the punishment often was absurd. Mississippi's infamous "pig law," for example, subjected hog thieves to up to five years in prison. The plantation owner would pick up his victims—many of them children under twelve—at the local courthouse, paying their fines in exchange for their services. Once on the farm, the offenders discovered that the cost of their upkeep exceeded the amounts of their fines. There was no way out. They had no one to turn to, no place to go. "The court and the man you work for are always partners," one victim explained. "One makes the fine, and the other one works you and holds you, and if you leave you are tracked with bloodhounds and brought back."

As might be expected when the law is used as an instrument of oppression, it is ignored as a restraining force. A spirit of lawlessness swept the land; black men—and women and children, too—were burned, shot, mutilated and hanged by mobs on the slightest pretense. Tuskegee Institute's records indicate that from 1882–1900 there were 3,011 lynchings—an average of one every other day. About 85 percent of the victims were black. The record also shows that the cause of most lynchings was "mistaken identity," "insult," "bad reputation," "unpopularity," "violating contracts," "running quarantine," "giving evidence" and similar actions. "It is a question whether when we go to work we will return or not," a black South Carolinian told the House of Representatives in 1901.

There was not even a law against lynching. The black man's only defense against a lynch mob was a rifle or fast feet—or both. In 1896 the Cleveland *Gazette* reported an encounter between a black man, Jack Trice, and a white mob in Palmetto, Florida. Trice's fourteen-year-old son had fought and beaten the son of Palmetto's Town Marshal. The next morning at 3 A.M. the Marshal and fourteen of his fellow citizens advanced on Trice's house and demanded the boy for punishment. Trice refused to give his son up, and the mob opened fire on the house. Returning their fire, Trice killed the Marshal with his first bullet. One man then advanced to burn the house, and Trice shot him in the head. Several others tried to batter in the door with a log; Trice mortally wounded one of them in the stomach. The mob, disheartened, broke and fled, and

Trice's deadly rifle dropped another one of them with a bullet in the back. A few hours later the survivors returned with reinforcements, but Trice and his son had fled.

The black postmaster of Lake City, South Carolina was not so fortunate. He had been threatened and shot at in attempts to make him leave his post. But he had replied by moving the post office into his house. "Being a government official," the Cleveland *Gazette* reported, "he felt confident of protection from Washington." It never came. In 1898, on George Washington's birthday, a mob of over 100 people set fire to his house and, as it burned, pumped volley after volley of bullets through the thin clapboard of the building. The postmaster was shot dead as he opened the door to flee the flames. His wife, following him, suffered several wounds; the baby she was carrying in her arms was killed. A second child was fatally wounded; two others were maimed. The house was burned to the ground, incinerating both the mail and the bodies of the postmaster and the infant.

When no action was taken to apprehend the murderers, Ida B. Wells, a black newspaperwoman, joined a delegation of Illinois congressmen to protest to President McKinley. Miss Wells was the foremost crusader for an antilynching law. Born in Mississippi in 1869, she had been forced at an early age to support her four younger sisters and brothers. She had succeeded, and had managed to put herself through college as well. After teaching for a time in Memphis, Tennessee, she had started her own newspaper, *Free Speech*. In 1892, after she had proved that the lynching of three successful black grocers had been incited by their white business rivals, a mob smashed her press, and she was forced to flee the city. She carried her crusade against lynching to northern cities and Europe. "If it were known that the Cannibals or the savage Indian had burned three human beings alive in the past two years," she wrote in 1894, "the whole of Christendom would be roused to devise ways and means to put a stop to it. Can you remain silent and inactive when such things are done in our own community and country?"

In her protest to President McKinley, Miss Wells emphasized that the Lake City case was a *federal* matter: a postmaster had been murdered and the mail destroyed. The government could not plead, as it usually did in lynch cases, that it was a state matter and therefore beyond its jurisdiction. Acting as a spokesman for a mass meeting of blacks, she asked the President for the apprehension of the killers, compensation for the postmaster's widow and children, and a national antilynching law.

The President replied that he was "in hearty accord" with the plea and that the Department of Justice and the Post Office Department would do what they could in the matter. Not surprisingly, that turned out to be nothing. The killers went unpunished, the widow remained uncompensated; no federal antliynching law ever was passed. George H. White of North Carolina, the last black congressman from the reconstruction, introduced an antilynching bill in the House in 1900. When he left Congress in 1901, he lamented that the bill "still sweetly sleeps" in the Judiciary Committee. One hundred thirty people were lynched that year.

As the twentieth century dawned, then, the black man was faced with poverty, discrimination and violence everywhere. Reformer Ray Stannard Baker, quoted Emerson's hymn to science: " 'To science there is no poison; to botany no weed; to chemistry no dirt.' To this," Baker observed drily, "we may add: 'to democracy no Negro.' "

There were attempts to stem the tide of black repression.

In 1890 northern Republicans in Congress introduced a bill for federal supervision of federal elections to protect the rapidly disappearing black voter. "If we fail to deal with this question rightly," the sponsor of the bill, Henry Cabot Lodge, told his colleagues, "we shall pay for it just as we paid the debt of slavery of which all this is a part." The bill, however, was filibustered to death in the Senate. Commenting on the defeat of the bill, *The New York Times* concluded: "No such measure will again be brought forward to embody a sentiment no longer existing or to revive slumbering fires."

In the South itself, the Populist party attempted to align poor blacks with poor whites against the established white power structure. The idea, explained Georgia's Tom Watson, the leading southern Populist, was to present a platform "immensely beneficial to both races and injurious to neither" and make it "to the interest of both races to act together for the success of the platform."

White farmers and black farmers each had formed their own organizations: the Southern Farmers' Alliance and the Colored Farmers' Alliance, the latter with more than a million members. "You are kept apart that you may be separately fleeced of your earnings," Watson explained to them. "You are made to hate each other because upon that hatred is rested the keystone of the arch of financial despotism which enslaves you both." The accident of color, he emphasized, "can make no difference in the interests of farmers, croppers and laborers." In 1892 both organizations threw their lots in with the national Populist party, which had been organized the previous year.

Combining with the Republicans, the Populists were able to defeat a number of Democratic conservatives in some southern states. In North Carolina, for example, the "Fusionists" won control of the state legislature in 1894 and elected both U.S. senators and a majority of representatives. Two years later they won the governorship as well. But their success was short-lived. The conservative Democrats split the blacks and whites by playing upon racist fears; where that was not enough, they resorted to violence and fraud. Nationally, the party was defused in 1896 by the Democrats, who adopted most of the Populist platform. By 1900 the Populists were an historical footnote.

Watson, blaming the blacks for the failure of the party, became a bitter racist and a Democrat in that order. In 1902, coming full circle, he wrote a popular treatise arguing that the black man was racially and culturally inferior and had contributed nothing to human progress. "What does civilization owe to the Negro race?" he asked. "Nothing! Nothing!! Nothing!!!" he concluded.

By this time the black man himself was thinking along those same lines. Despised and degraded, with neither dignity nor hope to hold him together, he was losing not only his political rights but also his identity—the sense of who he was, what he was worth. He was becoming the caricature the white man had made of him.

For a long time Frederick Douglass had provided standards to measure up to: pride, defiance, determination. But in his last years he had lost touch with the mass of blacks, and in 1895 he died.

A number of leaders had sprung up to carry on in the Douglass tradition, but they had been overshadowed by Booker T. Washington, a man more in step with his time. Appropriately enough, Washington had emerged as a leader in 1895, the same year that Douglass died. In retrospect it was a sad year for the black man, sadder than he knew.

Booker Taliaferro Washington was born in 1856 on a plantation in southern Virginia, the son of a black slave and a white man. As a slave he suffered the usual privations—hard work, little food, scant clothing and squalid quarters. Once freed, he and his brother and mother migrated about 150 miles northwest to Malden, West Virginia, a small Appalachian mining town where his stepfather had found work in a salt furnace. Young Booker was himself immediately put to work in the salt furnace and, later, in a coal mine.

Determined to get an education, Washington (a name he chose himself) studied relentlessly at night with an old spelling book and anyone who would tutor him. After several years in the mines, he was engaged as a houseboy by the mine owner's wife, a New England lady who instilled in him an everlasting reverence for cleanliness, order, propriety and industry. "Even to this day," Washington wrote in his autobiography thirty years later, "I never see bits of paper scattered around the house or in the street that I do not want to pick them up at once." And of the toothbrush he said: "I am convinced that there are few single agencies of civilization that are more far reaching."

At the age of seventeen he left Malden to attend Hampton Institute in Virginia, a vocational high school for blacks, which had been established by the Freedmen's Bureau during reconstruction. Arriving at Hampton hungry, dirty and ragged, he asked to be enrolled and was ordered to sweep one of the classrooms. "The sweeping of that room," he said later, "was my . . . examination." Being well versed in such skills, he passed easily and was accepted as a janitor and student.

Hampton was run by General S. C. Armstrong, a paternalistic New Englander, along military lines—regulated activities, strict schedule, daily rank and file inspection, proper manners and unquestioning conformity. Washington fit neatly into such a mold. In his autobiography he talks about a debating society he organized in addition to

Stairway of Treasurer's Residence. Students at Work. From *The Hampton Album* (1899-1900). Hampton was Booker T. Washington's alma mater. Collection The Museum of Modern Art, New York. Gift of Lincoln Kirstein.

the one he attended regularly every Saturday evening. "I noticed that between the time when supper was over and the time to begin evening study there were about twenty minutes which the young men usually spent in idle gossip. About twenty of us formed a society for the purpose of utilizing this time in debate or in practice in public speaking. Few persons ever derived more happiness or benefit from the use of twenty minutes of time than we did in this way."

Graduated with honors from Hampton in 1875, Washington spent the next four years teaching in Malden and studying in Washington, D.C. In 1879 he was invited to return to Hampton as a teacher and graduate student. His job was to supervise 75 Indians who had been brought to Hampton as an experiment in civilizing the "noble savage." In referring to the experiment, Washington reveals a rare skepticism of professional "do-gooders." He remarks that the Indians most resented having to cut their long hair and give up their traditional customs. "But no white American," he observes, "ever thinks that any other race is wholly civilized until he wears the white man's clothes, eats the white man's food, speaks the white man's language, and professes the white man's religion." Not until just before his death did Washington again show such perception.

In 1881 General Armstrong was asked to recommend someone to head a vocational school for blacks that was being organized at Tuskegee, deep in Alabama's agricultural "black belt." He suggested Washington. A telegram of acceptance came back, and Washington, who was only 25 years old, left for Tuskegee. When he arrived, he found nothing—no books, no building, not even any land. But he was industrious and ambitious, so he began to build the school himself. Probably nothing less would have satisfied him, for he measured success "not so much by the position that one had reached in life as by the obstacles which he has overcome while trying to succeed."

Washington was a persuasive fund raiser. Properly humble, he became a fashionable ornament in the drawing rooms of the rich. Within ten years Tuskegee had 450 students, fourteen buildings, more than 1,400 acres of farmland and an annual endowment of $20,000. "I believe," he said at one of the black conferences he held annually at Tuskegee, "if we do our duty in getting property, Christian education and character, in some way or another the sky will clear up, and we shall make our way onward."

He, at least, was making his way onward. In 1895 he was asked to speak at the opening of the Cotton States and International Exposition in Atlanta, the first black man so honored at such an event in the South. The Exposition contained an exhibition of black enterprise, and Washington, who was well known for his speaking ability and his comfortable views, had been chosen to represent enterprising blacks.

The day of the address, September 18, began with a three hour procession to the Exposition grounds under a burning sky. Arriving at the reception hall with the other dignitaries, Washington felt "ready to collapse." Thousands of people were milling outside the hall trying to enter; inside, the hall was packed to capacity. Taking his seat on the platform, Washington was cheered wildly by the blacks in the audience, faintly by the whites. Little did either of them know what awaited them.

He was scheduled to speak last. The strains of "Yankee Doodle" died out and were followed by mild cheers; then Washington was introduced by ex-Governor Rufus B. Bullock of Georgia as "a representative of Negro enterprise and Negro civilization."

The rays of the late afternoon sun shone level through the windows of the hall as Washington rose to speak. Tall and muscular, with a strong mouth and alert eyes, he might have been an athlete if he ever had taken the time to play at anything. Polite applause welcomed him. When it had subsided, he began what one historian recently described as "one of the most effective pieces of political oratory in the history of the United States."

He remarked how "the value and manhood of the American Negro" had been recognized by the Exposition, and that this recognition would "do more to cement the friendship of the two races than any occurrence since the dawn of our freedom." Then he asked the blacks to "cast down your buckets where you are"—with the friendly southern white man. A smattering of applause rose from the whites in the audience.

The blacks must learn "to glorify common labor," he suggested. "No race can prosper till it learns that there is as much dignity in tilling a field as in writing a poem. It is at the bottom of life we must begin, and not at the top." More applause. "Nor should we permit our grievances to overshadow our opportunities." Cheers.

Then he asked the whites to cast down their buckets among the blacks "whose habits you know, whose fidelity and love you have tested." If they did, he assured them, they would find themselves surrounded by "the most patient, faithful, law-abiding and unresentful people that the world has seen." Raising his hand above his head, with the fingers spread wide apart, he explained: "In all things that are purely social we can be as separate as the fingers, yet one as the hand in all things essential to mutual progress." This brought him a standing ovation.

The audience was his. After it quieted, he continued. The white man, he said, should encourage the development of the black man; the effort would pay "a thousand percent interest." And he added: "The wisest among my race understands that the agitation of questions of social equality is the extremist folly. . . . It is important and right that all privileges of the law be ours, but it is vastly more important that we be prepared for the exercises of these privileges." More cheers. "The opportunity to earn a dollar in a factory just now is worth infinitely more than the opportunity to spend a dollar in an opera house." Amens and cheers.

Concluding, he pledged the "patient, sympathetic help of my race" in bringing "into our beloved South a new heaven and a new earth." The audience leaped to its feet, shouting, whistling, applauding, waving canes and handkerchiefs. Governor Bullock rushed across the stage and wrung Washington's hand—the speech had succeeded beyond both men's expectations.

White America, relieved, immediately designated Washington the national spokesman of black America. The press, northern and southern, published the address and lavished praise upon it. President Grover Cleveland sent Washington his personal congratulations and later met with him. The Tuskegee educator was hailed as a "Negro Moses." If there were more Tuskegees and more Booker T. Washingtons, stated one Chicago editorial, "the race question would settle itself in ten years."

Received by presidents, consulted by congressmen, funded by millionaires, honored by Harvard, Booker T. Washington became one of the most influential men in the country. He set up what became known as the "Tuskegee Machine." W.E.B. Du Bois, one of Washington's severest critics, complained that "Tuskegee became a vast information bureau and center of advice. After a time almost no Negro institution could collect funds without the recommendation or acquiescence of Mr. Washington."

Washington's power, however, based as it was on his reflection of the white establishment's line, remained limited. He had to say pretty much what his sponsors wanted to hear. As Du Bois pointed out, Washington's dependence upon the charity of rich industrialists compelled him "to tell not the whole truth but that part of it which certain powerful interests in America wish to appear as the whole truth." Radical rhetoric would not produce dollars for Tuskegee from John D. Rockefeller.

"Actually Washington had no more faith in the white man than I do," Du Bois once said. But the Tuskegeean's theory was "When your head is in the lion's mouth, use your hand to pet him."

What Washington failed to see, however, was that, despite his petting—indeed, perhaps because of it—the black man was getting his head bitten off anyway. In 1906, Washington assured the blacks that they were living in a comparatively "happy period." That same year there were 65 lynchings—almost all of them of blacks—and major race riots in Atlanta, Georgia, Brownsville, Texas, and Greensburg, Indiana.

Washington either could not or would not see what was happening to the black man. He was neither intellectually nor emotionally broad enough to realize that the middle class virtues of propriety, industry and cleanliness were not enough to overcome more than two centuries of racism. A self-made man plastered over with the self-satisfaction of personal success, he was sure that his way should be everybody's way. He was the kind of man who, having exchanged a few platitudes with an English duchess at a reception and at Christmas having received "her photograph with her autograph on it," could count her as "one of our warmest friends."

Beneath the platitudes and the servility, however, some doubts about accommodation must have lingered, for in his last article Washington wrote that segregation did nothing for blacks but hold them back. In 1915, he died, closing an era that one historian has called "The Dark Ages of Recent American History."

"A new loyalty and allegiance replaced my Americanism. Henceforward I was a Negro."

W.E.B. Du Bois

BLACK AWAKENING

The death of Booker T. Washington left as the leading black American, W.E.B. Du Bois. Long a critic of Washington, Du Bois was in the tradition of Frederick Douglass. He believed in self-respect, political rights and equal opportunity—goals that the Tuskegeean had seemed willing to barter for second-class citizenship. The intellectual father of today's black militants, Du Bois set the tone of an emerging black protest and for almost half a century remained its strongest voice.

Writer, scholar, historian, editor, radical and, finally, political exile, William Edward Burghardt Du Bois was born in 1868 in Great Barrington, Massachusetts, a small mill town, that rests in the shadows of the Berkshire Mountains. He was a light-skinned black. In his autobiography, he explained proudly that his heritage included "a flood of Negro blood, a strain of French, a bit of Dutch, but thank God! no Anglo-Saxon."

Since his father drifted off shortly after his birth, Du Bois was reared by his mother's family, the Burghardts. They were typical New Englanders in every respect except color, so Du Bois learned to be thrifty, reserved, hard working, responsible and independent. In addition, his sensitivity and natural aloofness made him, in his own words, "nearly always the isolated outsider looking in." It gave him an insecurity that often passed for arrogance.

He was educated in the town's public schools, which were integrated. But he learned one of his most memorable lessons, as students so often do, outside the classroom. When he and his classmates bought and exchanged play visiting cards, he offered one of his cards to a white girl who, with a glance at him, refused it. "Then it dawned on me with a certain suddenness," he later recalled, "that I was different from the others . . . shut out from their world by a vast veil."

An outstanding student, Du Bois went on to college— one of only three or four (all whites) in his class who did. Some prominent citizens of the town raised a scholarship fund and sent him to Fisk University, a black college in Nashville, Tennessee. He later wrote about his introduction to southern customs, "No one but a Negro going into the South without previous experience of color caste can have any conception of its barbarism."

At Fisk, he edited the student newspaper, taught poor hill-country blacks and discovered the delights of Mozart. He was "thrilled" to find himself, for the first time, among a mass of black people. "A new loyalty and allegiance replaced my Americanism," he said of the experience. "Henceforward I was a Negro." Graduated from Fisk in 1888, he returned to New England resolved to be one of what he later called the "Talented Tenth"—black intellectuals who would lower the "color bar" and lead the black man to a "higher civilization."

He enrolled at Harvard to study philosophy and was graduated with honors in 1890. Two years later a grant enabled him to study economics, history and sociology in Germany. Traveling in Europe, he "became more human" and "learned the place in life of 'wine, women and song.' " And his studies convinced him that the "new social sciences" could be used to fight racism in America: one could define the problems through research, then formulate proposals for their solution.

Of his own role, he wrote in Germany on his twenty-fifth birthday: "I rejoice as a strong man to run a race. And I am strong—is it egotism or is it assurance? . . . O I wonder what I am—I wonder what the world is—I wonder if life is worth the striving. I do not know—perhaps I never shall know; but this I do know: be the Truth what it may, I shall seek it on the pure assumption that it is worth seeking. . . ." In 1894 he returned to the United States determined to make a name for himself in social science and in literature "and thus to raise my race."

His first opportunity to fulfill these ambitions came in 1896 when, under the auspices of the University of Pennsylvania, he did a sociological study of a black neighborhood in Philadelphia. The result was a book, *The Philadelphia Negro,* the first in-depth examination of life in a black urban ghetto. It set Du Bois to thinking. "I concluded," he said later, "that I did not know so much as I thought about my own people."

Determined to find out more, he conceived a broad program of sociological studies of problems affecting black Americans. From 1897 to 1914, as a teacher at Atlanta University and as director of the university's annual Atlanta Conference, Du Bois directed sixteen studies on such subjects as blacks in business, black family life and the black church. He later said of those years at Atlanta: "Here I found myself. . . . I became widely acquainted with the real condition of my people. I realized the terrific odds which faced them."

The Atlanta Conferences were to the urban black what Booker T. Washington's annual Tuskegee Negro Conferences were to the black farmer. At Atlanta, however, Du Bois emphasized science and social reform; while at Tuskegee, Washington stressed the benefits of "making it" through vocational education. In the beginning each man cooperated with the other, but as Washington's intolerance of other viewpoints increased, the gap between the two men widened until, in 1903, it became a chasm.

The occasion was the publication of Du Bois' *The Souls of Black Folk,* a collection of essays. Most notable was the one titled "Of Mr. Booker T. Washington and Others." In it, Du Bois described Washington's historic exposition speech in 1895 as the "Atlanta Compromise" and noted that the Tuskegeean's program "practically accepts the alleged inferiority of the Negro races." Du Bois opposed conciliation of the South on that basis. Instead he demanded for blacks the right to vote, civic equality and the education of youth according to ability.

The Souls of Black Folk, said writer James Weldon Johnson, had "a greater effect upon and within the Negro race in America than any other single book published in this country since *Uncle Tom's Cabin."* Its publication rallied together the more radical black intellectuals and agitators under Du Bois' leadership—a role which the Atlanta professor assumed reluctantly. As late as 1905 he still saw himself as "a scientist, and neither a leader nor an agitator." Washington, however, knew a heretic when he saw one and used all his powers to throttle his detractor. He persuaded the black press to vilify Du Bois and used his own influence among wealthy whites to reduce the flow of donations to Atlanta University and any organizations sympathetic to Du Bois. He even assigned informers to infiltrate such organizations.

Du Bois was no match for Washington while the Tuskegeean lived. Washington was a peerless organizer and skillful political infighter. A sound judge of men, he knew whom to flatter, whom to threaten, whom to reward, whom to punish; and he did it all in humble blackface. Du Bois had no taste for such activities. "I was no natural leader of men," he admitted. "I could not slap people on the back and make friends of strangers. I could not easily break down an inherited reserve; or at all times curb a biting, critical tongue."

He hated the role of being an activist leader. Always the professor, he preferred to lecture to a small group of intellectuals—the Talented Tenth—who might carry his message to the people. But the Talented Tenth didn't speak to the people either, which may help explain why Du Bois never gained the broad support that Malcolm X later enjoyed.

In 1905 Du Bois invited a number of the Talented Tenth to a summer conference near Buffalo, New York, to organize "aggressive action on the part of men who believe in Negro freedom and growth." Twenty-nine men responded, and in a little hotel on the Canadian side of the border (no hotel on the American side would accept blacks) the Niagara Movement was born. It was, says Du Bois' biographer Elliot M. Rudwick, "the first national organization of Negroes which aggressively and unconditionally demanded the same civil rights for their people which other Americans enjoyed."

But it was short-lived. Isolated from the white man's money by Washington and from the black man's support by the members' contempt for the people, the Niagara Movement petered out in 1910. Organized protest itself might have suffered the same fate had it not been for a vicious race pogrom in Springfield, Ohio, in 1908. There a white mob lynched two blacks, brutally assaulted scores of others and drove thousands more out of the city. Journalist William E. Walling's impassioned report of the event called for a "powerful body of citizens" to come to the blacks' aid. His call was answered by a radical young social worker, Mary White Ovington, who with Walling and others began to form such a body of citizens.

The following year the National Negro Committee was organized by white liberals. It included, besides Walling and Ovington, Rabbi Stephen S. Wise, reformer Jane Addams, and publisher Oswald Garrison Villard, grandson of abolitionist William Lloyd Garrison. Among the black committee members were Du Bois and several leaders of the faltering Niagara Movement.

The deliberations of the Committee were often heated. Some of the black members at times accused the white members of betraying them. Mary White Ovington perhaps summarized the attitude of the whites—an attitude that persists even today—when she said: "I find myself still occasionally forgetting that the Negroes aren't poor people for whom I must kindly do something, and then comes a gathering such as that last evening and I learn they are men with most forceful opinions of their own."

In 1910 the Committee became the National Association for the Advancement of Colored People. The NAACP dedicated itself to securing for blacks "justice in the courts, education for their children, employment according to their ability, and complete equality before the law." Attorney Moorefield Storey, a former secretary to Charles Sumner, was elected National President; and Du Bois, the new Association's only black officer, was appointed Director of Publications and Research. Du Bois resigned his position at Atlanta University giving as his reason the loss of white financial aid caused, he knew, by his presence there. "My career as a scientist," he said, "was to be swallowed up in my role as master of propaganda."

For the next 34 years Du Bois' principal vehicle of propaganda was *Crisis,* the Association's monthly magazine, which he founded and edited. In it he encouraged black writers and artists, lectured the black bourgeoisie, and denounced the white establishment. He conceived of *Crisis* as "an independent organ leading a liberal organization toward radical reform." But in this program he failed. His ideas were too radical for the NAACP leadership. And he wanted more power and independence for blacks than paternalistic white liberals were willing to concede to them.

This provoked a running battle between Du Bois and the Association's white leadership. The militant editor was characterized by Villard as "a very great asset" but also "a danger." Mary White Ovington, in words still pertinent today, again put the situation in focus. She called it "a confession to the world that we cannot work with colored people unless they are our subordinates."

In 1926 Du Bois visited Russia and returned a convinced Bolshevik. Having been influenced by Karl Marx's theories some years before, he now became more openly Marxist. When the nation's economy collapsed in the Great Depression, he reaffirmed his belief in Marx's program of redistribution of income, state-owned industry, and universal education. He did not, however, join the Communist party, believing it to be insufficiently aware of race prejudice.

Meanwhile, Du Bois was at odds with Walter White, who in 1931 had become the Association's National Secretary. Du Bois did not agree with the fair-skinned White, whom he accused of being more white than black, and resented White's efforts to control *Crisis.* The long battle with the NAACP leadership now came to a showdown. The immediate issue was Du Bois' advocacy of a "segregated economy"—a kind of "black power" in which blacks would plan and control economic activity in the black community. The leadership refused to endorse it, and Du Bois resigned from the NAACP in 1934. He was 66 years old.

He returned to Atlanta University where he attempted, without much success, to revive his sociological studies of blacks. In 1940 he founded *Phylon,* "a quarterly magazine to record the situation of the colored world and guide its course of development." But four years later he was suddenly "retired" by the university. "Without a word of warning," Du Bois later wrote, "I found myself at the age of 76 without employment and with less than $5,000 in savings."

The NAACP offered him a job as director of special research. He accepted it. But he still was too radical and too independent for the Association, and in 1948 he was dismissed for refusing to "cooperate" with White. He then became an honorary Vice Chairman of the Council on African Affairs, an organization that the United States Attorney General had listed as "subversive."

Du Bois long had been involved in the Pan-African Movement. He had been an official at the first Pan-African Conference in 1900 in London. It was there he had observed, prophetically: "The problem of the Twentieth Century is the problem of the color line. . . ." And in 1905 he had predicted a general race war unless whites reformed.

In 1919 he had organized his own Pan-African Congress in Paris under the sponsorship of the NAACP. Demanding "justice . . . and economic and social equality according to ability" for all "persons of African descent," Du Bois had described the Congress as the beginning of a worldwide race movement. But subsequent Congresses in 1921 and 1923 had generated little enthusiasm; and a spiritless conclave in 1927 had been the last Congress until 1945.

The Council on African Affairs had not fared much better, but Du Bois lent it the luster of his name. He also involved himself with peace groups, which were protesting against the Cold War, the worldwide struggle for power between the Soviet Union and the United States. Praising the Russians, he accused the United States of "leading the world to hell in a new colonialism. . . ." In 1950, as the American Labor Party's candidate for U. S. Senator from New York, he campaigned against the Korean War. He lost, of course. The following year, he was indicted by the government for refusing to register "as an agent of a foreign principal." The indictment referred to his work for the Peace Information Center, another organization on the Attorney General's subversive list.

The mood of the 1950's was violently anticommunist, and anyone who viewed the Soviet Union as anything but a threat to the "free world," or who simply opposed the nation's rigid anti-Soviet policies was labeled a communist, a subversive, or both. Richard Nixon rode roughshod into the vice-presidency on this hysteria. Wisconsin's Senator Joseph R. McCarthy created an American Inquisition with lists of people he described as communist spies. "I have here in my hand a list of 205 that were known to the Secretary of State . . ." he would announce. The numbers changed constantly, but the communist spies never materialized. McCarthyism, however, turned American against American and, with few exceptions, muffled the voices of dissent.

Du Bois was acquitted of the government's charge in court, but he remained branded by the stigma of accusation. After the trial he was shunned by colleges and publishers, harassed by the government, and repudiated even by the NAACP. "It was a bitter experience, and I bowed before the storm," he later wrote. "But I did not break."

In effect, however, his public career was over. The next ten years he spent writing and traveling, visiting the Soviet Union and China and enthusiastically praising their spirit and accomplishments. In 1961 he joined the Communist Party. Later that year, almost totally alienated from American society, he went to live in Ghana, becoming a Ghanaian citizen. In 1963, at the age of 95, he died in Accra.

At the end Du Bois was a total protester, having renounced the social, political and economic structure of the land of his birth. His progression to this position is instructive because it parallels the experience of many contemporary blacks who, in less time of course, have made the same journey.

At first Du Bois only wanted into the white world. "What the white world was doing, its goals and ideals, I had not doubted were quite right," he admitted. "What was wrong was that I and people like me . . . who might have my ability and aspirations were refused permission to be a part of this world It was as though moving on a rushing express, my main thought was as to my relations with the other passengers on the express, and not to its rate of speed and it destination."

As Du Bois gradually became aware of the nature and destination of the express, he rejected them. Finally, he left the train, hoping it could be rerouted. It didn't matter that the train he switched to was no better than the one he had left. Du Bois simply was more reliable in what he rejected than in what he embraced.

Du Bois' involvement with the NAACP touched upon only one aspect of its activities: propaganda and protest.

The Association also lobbies in Washington and in many state capitals for civil rights legislation. And it maintains a separate, independent Legal Defense Fund, which presses the fight against discrimination through the courts. "Judicial rights and legislative approval, that's our continuing fight," says the Association's present Executive Director, Roy Wilkins.

The Association's legal activities—an operation that was adopted from the Niagara Movement—have helped make the black man, in Wilkins' words, a "legal entity." Indeed, in the Association's early years, the courts were its only recourse. Southern conservatives in Congress effectively blocked civil rights legislation, and the White House was content to drift with the time. "Segregation is not humiliating but a benefit, and ought to be so regarded by you gentlemen," President Woodrow Wilson told a group of black leaders; and his Republican successors offered blacks little more than pious platitudes.

The NAACP's first court case involved a New Jersey black who had been arrested for murder. "There was no evidence against him," recalled Mary White Ovington, "but he was black and had been near the scene of the crime." The Association won his release.

Within a few years NAACP lawyers, both black and white, were winning vital test cases before the Supreme Court. In 1915 they helped overturn Oklahoma's "grandfather clause," a law that barred blacks from voting by requiring all voters to have voted prior to 1867 or to be the sons or grandsons of such voters. Two years later NAACP lawyers won a verdict declaring unconstitutional a Louisville, Kentucky, law that forbade blacks to buy property on a block where the majority of property owners were white. Choosing its court tests carefully, the NAACP was also successful in eliminating the white primary, in securing more equal educational facilities for blacks and, in 1954, in outlawing segregated public education altogether. Thurgood Marshall, since 1966 a Supreme Court Associate Justice, was for 25 years a special counsel for the Association's Legal Defense Fund. In that time he argued 32 cases before the high court and won 29 of them.

After the 1954 school desegregation decision, the Association's membership almost doubled. It currently stands near the half million mark. Most of the members are educated, middle class and moderate—a description that also fits their leader, Roy Wilkins.

Born in 1901 in St. Louis, Wilkins went to school in St. Paul, Minnesota, was graduated from the state university and for several years edited a black weekly in Kansas City, Missouri. In 1931 he became Walter White's assistant at the Association's headquarters in New York. When White died in 1955, Wilkins succeeded him.

Like his predecessor, Wilkins has a sure feel for the politics of power. "The Negro has to be a superb diplomat and a great strategist," he has said. "He has to parlay what actual power he has along with the good will of the white majority. He has to devise and pursue those philosophies and activities which will least alienate the white majority opinion."

Views like these have earned Wilkins the contempt of many black activists and radicals who see him—and the NAACP—as "irrelevant" to the black man's need to establish his identity and independence. Wilkins himself admits that the Association has a lot of catching up to do, especially in the urban ghettos, where 75 percent of American blacks now live.

The NAACP now is trying harder in the ghettos, sponsoring leadership programs and low-income housing. Fittingly, if belatedly, it is turning to those people—urban blacks—whose persecution by whites was largely responsible for the formation of the Association in the first place.

The urban ghettos originally were created by the large-scale migrations of southern blacks, which began with the Great Exodus of 1879. Most of the "exodusters," however, went to Kansas and Nebraska, where they continued to lead essentially rural lives. Migrations to northern and eastern urban centers did not begin to reach massive proportions until 1910 and after, when blacks were driven from the farms by poverty and oppression and the lure of jobs in the big cities.

"i am in the darkness of the south and i am trying to get out . . ." one Alabaman wrote in 1917 to the Chicago *Defender,* a widely circulated newspaper that encouraged migration. "i am counted no more thin a dog help me please help me o . . . i mean business i work if i can get a good job."

The jobs were there. World War I had created an industrial boom and at the same time shut off the flow of European immigrants who otherwise would have supplied the cheap labor to man the assembly lines. Northern employers sought black laborers, the *Defender* noted, "because it was either the black workmen or no workmen at all, and between the two evils they wisely chose to have workmen."

Most migrants gravitated to the four cities that today have the largest black populations in the country: New York, Chicago, Philadelphia and Detroit. But they also settled in Cleveland, Buffalo, Indianapolis, Gary, Pittsburgh, Milwaukee and Boston. During World War II, a new generation headed West, where they made the black population of Los Angeles the sixth largest in the nation.

Once in the cities, the migrants were herded into slum

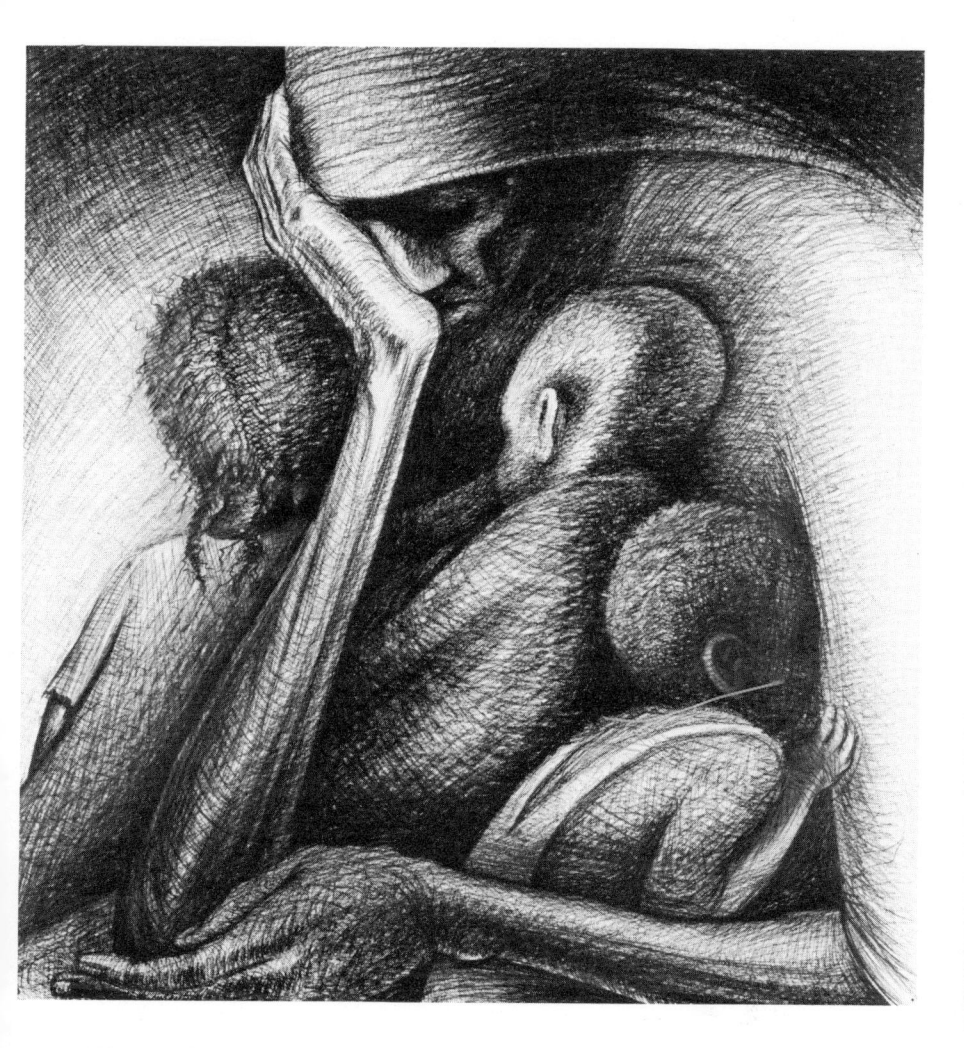

The Cradle. Drawing by John Biggers. The Museum of Fine Arts, Houston.

neighborhoods, sometimes by discriminatory laws, more often by private agreement among white property owners and rental agents. In every city a "Harlem" sprung up. And, in every one, conditions were similar. The black man was jammed into rotting, rat-infested buildings, cheated by white-owned businesses and assaulted both by criminals and by policemen. His children died from disease and malnutrition at three and four times the rate that white children did, and those who survived were sent to run-down, overcrowded schools where they were scorned, neglected or bored to death.

Outside the ghetto, everything was segregated. Jackie Robinson, the major leagues' first black baseball player, remembering his boyhood in Pasadena, California, in the 1920's, said: "We saw movies from segregated balconies, swam in the municipal pool only on Tuesdays and were permitted in the YMCA on only one night a week. Restaurant doors were slammed in our faces."

Even inside the ghetto, the black man found certain doors shut against him. During the Harlem "renaissance" of the 1920's, for example, when the work of black artists and writers came into vogue and Harlem nightclubs became a white tourist attraction, the most fashionable of these white-owned clubs excluded blacks.

And, if a black man attempted to break out of the ghetto, he was certain to meet resistance. In Detroit, in 1925, Dr. Ossian Sweet bought a home in a middle-class white neighborhood. Shortly after the purchase was announced, he was threatened with death and destruction if he moved in. Racial antagonism, with violence as its expression, had been inflamed by a revived Ku Klux Klan, which had arisen in Georgia in 1915. Denouncing Catholics, Jews, Orientals and "radicals" as well as blacks, the new Klan had a greater following outside the South than within it. Indeed, the

Grand Dragon of the 500,000 member Indiana Klan could say: "I am the law in Indiana."

Dr. Sweet waited nine months before moving, giving his would be neighbors time to adjust to the idea of a black man on the block. Then he moved in. A crowd immediately gathered in front of his home. The next day the crowd grew to a mob. But Dr. Sweet had anticipated trouble and had brought with him guns and ammunition and some friends and relatives to use them. More friends arrived on the second day, and the mob ominously followed them to the front door.

"It looked like a human sea," Sweet said later. He let his friends in and shut the door. "I had my back against the wall," he said. "I was filled with a peculiar fear, the fear of one who knows the history of my race. I knew what mobs had done to my race before."

Shots rang out from the street, and they were answered by firing from Sweet's upstairs window. In the exchange, a white man fell dead in the street, another was wounded. Having done nothing to disperse the mob, the police now arrested everyone in the house and charged them with murder.

The NAACP hired famed lawyer Clarence Darrow to defend the Sweets. In his summation to the jury he pointed out that if white men had killed a black man while protecting a home and family from a mob "no one would have dreamed of having them indicted. . . . They would have been given medals instead." The jury agreed and brought back a verdict of acquittal.

While the NAACP was battling for equal rights in the courts, another interracial organization, the Urban League, was helping rural blacks adjust to their new urban surroundings. Like the NAACP, the League originally had been conceived of and led by white liberals. In 1911 they had merged three existing social service organizations to form the National League on Urban Conditions Among Negroes. The League, its charter stated, would seek "not alms but opportunity."

In its early years, the League trained social workers, conducted studies of economic and social conditions among urban blacks and tried to find jobs for blacks. It still does all these things and more, but its emphasis today is on placing blacks in jobs.

Like the NAACP, the League works from within the white power structure. The nature of the League makes it almost imperative that it do so. Many of its projects are financed by corporate grants and federal funds, and the jobs it seeks must come from the business community.

The man who set the League on its present course and who for ten years was its Executive Director was Whitney M. Young, Jr. Born in 1921 in Lincoln Ridge, Kentucky, Young grew up in a solid, middle-class home. His father was the president of Lincoln Institute, a school for blacks, and his mother was the first black postmistress in the country. A good student, Young earned high grades and degrees at two colleges. He also discovered he could deal effectively with white people. During World War II, while taking an intensive course at the Massachusetts Institute of Technology, he roomed with a white Mississippian. At first his roommate refused even to speak to him, but within six months he had asked Young to be best man at his wedding.

After the war, Young lectured at colleges, worked for Urban League groups in St. Paul, Minnesota, and in Omaha, Nebraska, then served as dean of Atlanta University's School of Social Work. In 1961, assured by the League's Board of Directors that they would back him in making the organization more "militant," he accepted its directorship.

The League was plodding along; Young made it more aggressive. He emphasized "equality" rather than "improvement," set up a separate Washington bureau to obtain federal funds, and organized League affiliates throughout the South. In 1963 he called for a "Domestic Marshall Plan" to be financed by the Federal Government over a ten-year period. Blacks, he explained, suffered a "discrimination gap," which had been caused by "more than three centuries of abuse, humiliation, segregation and bias." They needed "more-than-equal" treatment to enable them to compete with whites in the job market. The idea was paid considerable lip service (a few years later) but it attracted no federal funds.

Undismayed, Young continued to press for massive public and private programs for blacks in education, housing and job training. "It's sheer economics, sheer common sense . . ." he insisted. "We will either help Negroes to become constructive, productive citizens—or they will become destructive dependents."

Early in 1971 Young died suddenly while visiting Nigeria, leaving behind him an organization that, like the NAACP, is often dismissed as irrelevant by many black militants. Young himself resented the charge of irrelevancy. He felt that getting work for people was relevant. But relevancy is an elusive quality and can disappear quickly. The League's emphasis on jobs, for example, was futile during the 1930's when there simply were no jobs to be had.

The Great Depression was hard on everyone, but hardest on the black man. He had been the last to be hired; now he was the first to be fired. In 1934 more than half the black families in northern cities, more than a third in southern cities, were on relief. The corresponding figure for whites was 10 to 13 percent. In Pittsburgh, blacks constituted only 8 percent of the population but almost 40 percent of the unemployed.

"He worked in the steel mills for four, five years and was a good man," one Pittsburgh housewife with six children said of her husband. "The mill closed, and he was laid off. He went out early every morning and walked the streets until night, looking for work. Day after day he done this . . . Once a man told him that he needn't trouble looking for a job as long as there is so many white men out of work."

In such circumstances, the Urban League was powerless. Indeed, so was the business community upon which the League depends. More radical programs were needed. And President Franklin D. Roosevelt inaugurated them in the New Deal. Agencies such as the Civilian Conservation Corps (CCC), the Works Projects Administration (WPA) and the Tennessee Valley Authority (TVA) put people to work. To be sure, the usual discrimination found its way into all these agencies—blacks were paid less and given dirtier jobs—but at the time any job was better than none.

As usual, the southern black agricultural worker suffered most. Caught not only in the general economic collapse but in a pernicious sharecropping system as well, he sank to a new level of despair. "If it wasn't the boll weevil it was the drought," one farmer said; "if it wasn't the drought it was the rains. . . . What kills us here is that we jest can't make it 'cause they pay us nothing for what we give them, and they charge us double price when they sell it back to us."

On a sultry July evening in 1934, 27 sharecroppers, black and white, met in a rickety Arkansas schoolhouse to consider forming a union to protect themselves against such practices. The question of whether to have two segregated unions or a single integrated one arose. An old black sharecropper who had seen his black union wiped out by armed whites in 1919 stood up to speak.

"For a long time now," he said, "the white folks and the colored folks have been fighting each other and both of us has been getting whipped all the time. . . . It won't do no good for us to divide because there's where the trouble has been all the time. The landlord is always betwixt us, beatin' us and starvin' us, and makin' us fight each other. There ain't but one way for us to get him where he can't help himself, and that's fer us to get together and stay together."

The same oppression that had united white and black farmers in the Populist party in the 1890's now unified these sharecroppers. They formed a single integrated organization, the Southern Tenant Farmer's Union, even though some of the whites were former members of the Ku Klux Klan. At the height of its power, the STFU numbered about 31,000 members in Arkansas, Mississippi, North Carolina and some of the border states. But harassment, intimidation and murder by planters and local "law" officers blunted the Union's effectiveness, and the end of the Depression finally killed it.

The Depression itself dragged on through the 1930's. Before it was really over, Adolph Hitler had conquered most of Europe, Franklin Roosevelt had won a third term as President, and American industry had turned to the production of war materials.

The boom in war production finally ended the Depression—for the white worker. For the black worker, it was the same old story: traditional discrimination effectively excluded him from the defense industries. "Regardless of their training as aircraft workers," declared the president

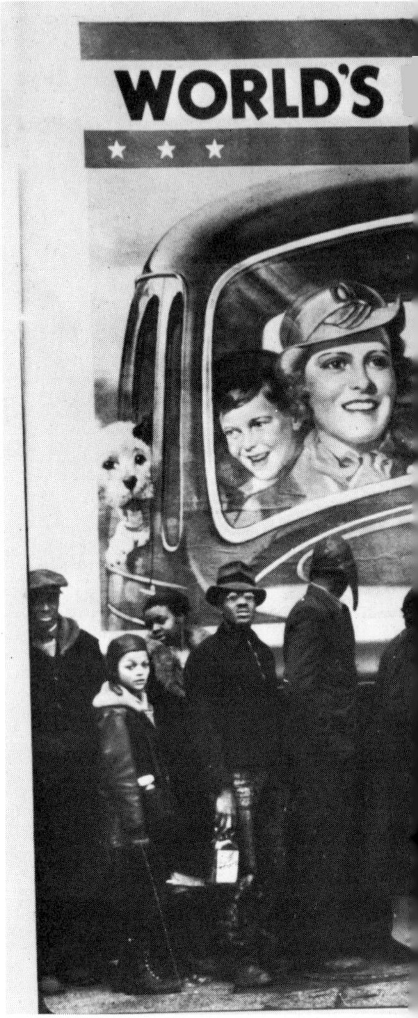
WORLD'S

Louisville Flood, 1937. Photograph by Margaret Bourke-White.
Life Magazine © Time, Inc.

of North American Aviation Company in the spring of 1941, "we will not employ Negroes in the North American plant. It is against company policy." Of 30,000 defense workers in New York City, less than 150—one-half of one percent—were black.

Black leaders appealed to Roosevelt to issue an executive order prohibiting racial discrimination in defense industries. Roosevelt had been the first Democrat to attract masses of black voters, largely through his New Deal policies and his deliberate wooing of minorities—the blacks, the immigrants, the poor. He had created a civil rights section in the Justice Department. But when pressed to do more, he pleaded that southern committee chairmen tied his hands. "If I come out for the antilynching bill now," he had told the NAACP's Walter White in 1935, "they will block every bill I ask Congress to pass to keep America from collapsing. I just can't take that risk." The Depression over, black leaders were again asking him to take that risk.

But Roosevelt marked time. Conferences and consultations were held—still no order was issued. Finally, in the spring of 1941, labor leader A. Philip Randolph concluded: "The Administration will never give the Negro justice until they see masses—ten, twenty, fifty thousand Negroes on the White House lawn." He called for a mass march on Washington.

If anyone could rally a mass of blacks to the capital, it was Asa Philip Randolph, who had been doing the improbable since his birth in Crescent City, Florida, in 1889. The son of a poor minister, Randolph had left home early to attend Florida's only high school for blacks, Cookman Institute in Jacksonville. His father had sent him off with two books as guides: the *Bible* and *The Souls of Black Folk*.

He worked his way through Cookman by digging ditches and laying cross ties on the new railroad down the Florida east coast. When his schooling and the railroad had been completed, he migrated to New York City. Arriving with the worn copy of Du Bois's book in his pocket and little else, he walked into a luxury apartment building and asked the superintendent for a job. He was hired to sweep the sidewalk and mop the halls.

For the next seven years, he worked as a porter, elevator boy, cook and waiter, while taking evening courses in economics, political science, philosophy, writing and public speaking. He had trouble holding jobs because he always tried to unionize his fellow workers, which made him unpopular with employers. One evening in 1915, unemployed again, he was having coffee in a Harlem cafeteria with a young law student, Owen Chandler. The two friends discussed what they could do with their lives and decided to begin publishing a magazine that would reach black workers. "Negroes must be free in order to be equal," Randolph insisted, "and they must be equal in order to be free." That became the message of *The Messenger*.

Randolph and Chandler preached militancy, action. "The colored people of America want . . . political, economic and social equality," they wrote. "Will this come? It will only come if the downtrodden people fight for it." They quoted Frederick Douglass (who had lifted it from the 19th century English poet, Lord Byron): "Who would be free, themselves must strike the blow."

The Messenger denounced white institutions and anyone who appeared to accommodate them. Not even Du Bois, Randolph's boyhood inspiration, escaped the editors' wrath. In 1918, while World War I still raged, Du Bois wrote a famous *Crisis* editorial called "Closed Ranks." Although racial segregation and discrimination continued, both at home and in the armed forces overseas, Du Bois advised blacks to "forget our special grievances" and fight "shoulder to shoulder" with whites, making this sacrifice "gladly and willingly with our eyes lifted to the hills." This "infamous" editorial, wrote the *Messenger* editors, would "rank in shame and reeking disgrace with the 'Atlanta Compromise' speech of Booker Washington." The duty of blacks, they said, was not to close ranks but to overturn American institutions. Revolution was "the only hope of the Negro as well as of mankind."

Randolph, by now a socialist, ran for New York State Controller on the Socialist party ticket in 1920. He lost. But he continued to try to unionize workers. With the help of *The Messenger,* he finally succeeded in organizing an elevator operators' union. Then, in 1925, the porters and maids who worked on the Pullman railroad cars asked him to help them organize. He accepted and made *The Messenger* the spokesman of the new Brotherhood of Sleeping Car Porters and Maids.

Of course, getting the Pullman Company to recognize the new union was another matter. For almost twelve years, company officials bitterly resisted the idea of a union. Randolph persisted. Finally, company officials sent him a check for $5,000 with a polite note suggesting that he and his wife might enjoy a hard-earned vacation abroad. Randolph didn't have the rent money for that month, but he sent the check back. A few months later the company capitulated and signed a contract with the Brotherhood.

The Brotherhood became an affiliate of the American Federation of Labor (AFL), a federation of unions of skilled workers. Most AFL unions either excluded or segregated blacks. Randolph, the first black man to sit on the Federation's executive board, immediately began prodding the other labor leaders to discontinue these practices. He was helped by the pressure created by the formation in 1938 of the rival Congress of Industrial Organization (CIO), a federation of unions of unskilled and semiskilled workers, black and white. But in 1941 the black worker still was effectively excluded from most jobs—either by the unions or by management.

Randolph was determined that the black man get his share of work. He was not going to advise him to put his shoulder to a wheel that would grind him under. "We are loyal, patriotic Americans, all," he wrote in his call to the march on Washington. But "if American democracy will not give jobs to its toilers because of race or color . . . it is a hollow mockery and belies the principles for which it is supposed to stand."

The March on Washington Movement, as the project was named, was called anarchistic, communistic, subversive, seditious. Still, Randolph pressed on with it. Roosevelt asked him to call it off. He refused. The day of the march drew near and estimates of the number of marchers who were preparing to descend on Washington ran from 10,000 to 100,000. Roosevelt, convinced that the prospects of a march were real, summoned Randolph, Walter White of the NAACP, and T. A. Hill of the Urban League to the White House. The result was Executive Order 8802, creating the Fair Employment Practices Committee (FEPC), issued four days before the march was scheduled to take place. It was the first time since reconstruction that the federal government had intervened on behalf of the black man.

Roosevelt's order was hailed by some as a second Emancipation Proclamation. Actually, the real significance of the entire episode lay in the success of the Movement; the FEPC itself had little enforcement power and was killed in 1946 by southern congressmen. But the Movement, as

Randolph said, was "the first demonstration on a national scale of the faith of the Negro people in themselves, their own capacity to win their rights against opposition."

The Movement continued to agitate for an end to racial discrimination and segregation in America. Among other things, Randolph wanted to make the FEPC a permanent agency (its dissolution in 1946 proved the wisdom of this demand), and to see minority groups represented on all administrative agencies. He also repeated an earlier demand: the abolition of segregation in the armed forces.

Pearl Harbor made this last demand an urgent issue. At the beginning of the war, blacks were excluded from the Air Force and Marines, and restricted to menial service tasks in the Navy; and, of course, in every branch they were segregated. Humiliated, slighted, beaten, sometimes murdered, the black serviceman became increasingly bitter about fighting to save the world for a democracy that did not apply to him. "Just carve on my tombstone," said one soldier, " 'Here lies a black man killed fighting a yellow man for the protection of a white man.' "

The armed forces remained segregated throughout the war, except for a brief period during the Battle of the Bulge when volunteers were needed to stem the German counterattack and blacks were integrated into white fighting units. After the Germans were halted, segregation was restored.

In 1946, President Harry S. Truman created a presidential Committee on Civil Rights to investigate postwar racial discrimination and to recommend a program for racial justice. "The pervasive gap between our aims and what we actually do," the Committee reported, "is creating a kind of moral dry rot, which eats away at the emotional and rational bases of democratic beliefs." An end to segregation in education, employment, housing and public services—including the armed services—was recommended.

Truman included some of the Committee's proposals in his legislative recommendations to Congress in 1948, but desegregation of the armed forces was not one of them. Randolph then called for civil disobedience, advising blacks to resist the draft until the armed forces were desegregated. A few months later Truman issued Executive Order 9981, abolishing such segregation.

In the interim, Randolph was questioned by a Senate committee regarding the extent of his program of civil disobedience. He was asked if he would counsel draft resistance even if the nation were attacked. Yes, he replied, because it was the only way "to make America wake up and realize that we do not have a democracy here as long as one black man is denied all of the rights enjoyed by all the white men in this country."

The battle had been joined.

Revolution

Regular organized protest by blacks began in the 1940's. Randolph's threat of a march on Washington was enough to persuade Roosevelt to create the FEPC in 1941. The following year, CORE held its first sit-in, in Chicago. In 1943 serious race riots—the most violent form of protest—broke out in Detroit and New York. And the first brief freedom ride (then called a "journey of reconciliation") was launched in 1947.

The next two decades produced a black revolution of increasing intensity. First, activists like Martin Luther King, Jr., James Farmer, John Lewis and Bayard Rustin organized strikes, sit-ins, freedom rides, marches and voter registration drives. New organizations like the Southern Christian Leadership Conference and the Student Nonviolent Coordinating Committee were formed; old ones like the Congress of Racial Equality, the NAACP and the Urban League were revitalized. Then, militants like Stokely Carmichael, Malcolm X, Huey Newton and Eldridge Cleaver preached black nationalism, black power and black studies and organized the black community for self-defense. The Black Panthers were born, the Black Muslims were revived and activist organizations like SNCC and CORE became more militant.

The black revolution began in 1954, the year the Supreme Court declared segregation of public schools unconstitutional. Some white southerners refused to comply with the decision, and in 1957 President Eisenhower dispatched federal troops to Little Rock, Arkansas, to enforce the law. Meanwhile, the black man himself, aided by some whites, took direct, nonviolent action to secure his rights. In 1956 King led the Montgomery, Alabama, bus strike. Four years later, black students began a wave of sit-ins for integration. In 1961 the sit-ins were followed by freedom rides and voter registration drives, and in 1963 by a mass march on Washington. The legislative fruits of these activities were the Civil Rights Act of 1964 and the Voting Rights Act of 1965.

But 1965 also was the year of the Watts rebellion and of Malcolm X's assassination. In 1966 black power, black studies and the Black Panthers were born. A year later, Newark and Detroit exploded in violence, and in 1968 King was killed.

Change followed change, but one thing remained constant: after 1954 the black man refused to accept an inferior status. A new resolve and new self-respect took shape, new leaders and new attitudes emerged. Demonstrating, marching, rebelling, the black man placed white America on notice that the time for waiting for equality was over.

"We want our colored people to go on living like they have for the last 100 years."

*Sheriff Z. T. Matthews,
Terrell County, Georgia*

THE FIGHT TO INTEGRATE

In late 1948, while black leaders girded for the next round of battles, the white power structure began showing signs of internal strain over the civil rights issue. President Truman's request for extended civil rights legislation had deepened the rift between northern and southern Democrats that had been developing since Roosevelt's Administration. Then, reluctantly nominated by the Democrats in 1948, Truman further alienated the southern conservative wing of the party by insisting upon a strong civil rights "plank" in the party platform. Hoping their defection would cost Truman the election, some of these southerners started a third party, the Dixiecrats, and ran their own candidate for President, J. Strom Thurmond of South Carolina, a hard-line segregationist.

To everyone's surprise, Truman won the election. But, blocked by southern conservatives in Congress, he was unable to produce any civil rights legislation. Meanwhile, black leaders carried forward a struggle for equality in the courts.

In the late 1930's the Supreme Court had become the principal agent of reform in the area of civil rights. The Court had been extending to civil rights the protection that in an earlier era it had reserved for property rights. In 1944 it struck down the white primary in Texas. Two years later it prohibited segregation in interstate buses. And two years after that it forbade discriminatory restrictions in the sale of private property.

The NAACP's legal division kept the pressure on, and the Court continued to strike down discriminatory laws. In 1950 it ruled against segregated trains; in 1954, against segregated schools. Of this last decision, *Brown* v. *Board of Education of Topeka, The New York Times* said: "Probably no decision in the history of the Court has directly concerned so many individuals."

Actually, the decision very nearly went the other way, despite the unanimous final vote. Before the Court ruled officially, the Justices discussed the case privately and split 5 to 4 in favor of segregation. Then Chief Justice Frederik M. Vinson, one of the minority, died in September 1953, and Earl Warren, a former Governor of California, was appointed his successor. Quietly, privately, Warren personally persuaded the majority of Justices, one by one, to change their votes. The result was an historic unanimous decision. But had not fate intervened, history might have taken a different turn.

The *Brown* decision had special significance, because the segregated school was an important symbol to white southerners. Even during reconstruction southern schools were integrated only in two states, and there only fitfully and fleetingly. At the time of the Court's decision, segregated schools were required by law in seventeen southern and border states and in Washington, D.C., and they were common in three other states. Altogether, 40 percent of the nation's public school children were segregated by law.

More than any other single factor, segregated schools had helped perpetuate the myth of the black man's racial and cultural inferiority. Segregation had been sanctioned by the Court in 1896, in the *Plessy* v. *Ferguson* ruling which established the principle of "separate but equal" facilities. But, in fact, the segregated educational facilities never had been equal. "There has never been any serious attempt in this state to offer adequate educational facilities for the colored race," a white school superintendent in Mississippi admitted in 1912. As late as 1930, for every $2 spent for a black child in the South, $7 was spent for a white child. And in 1954, the year of the Court's decision, the ratio was $10 for a black child, $13 for a white one. "We conclude," stated Chief Justice Earl Warren, speaking for the Court, "that in the field of public education the doctrine of 'separate but equal' has no place. Separate educational facilities are inherently unequal."

In the border states and in the District of Columbia, some integration quickly followed the Court's decision; but in the states of the old Confederacy, politicians looked for ways to circumvent the decision. "I shall use every legal means at my command," said Virginia's Governor Thomas B. Stanley, "to continue segregated schools in Virginia." Governor Herman Talmadge of Georgia declared that his state would "not tolerate the mixing of the races in the public schools or any other tax-supported institutions." Except in a few districts in Texas, it took federal court orders to compel school integration in the deep South.

In 1955 the Supreme Court spoke again. To foil the legal delaying tactics of segregationists, it ruled that all school districts must be desegregated "with all deliberate speed." Virginia's answer to that in 1956 was a program of "Massive Resistance" to desegregation—laws that cut off state aid to desegregated schools, forcing them to close. A month later, 101 members of Congress from the deep South signed a "Southern Manifesto," pledging "to use all lawful means to bring about a reversal of this decision which is contrary to the Constitution." School integration virtually came to a halt.

Although it cautioned against "disorder and unlawful acts," the Southern Manifesto inspired many hard-core segregationists to take the law into their own hands. The Ku Klux Klan flared up again, and White Citizens' Councils and other Klanlike organizations sprang up throughout the South. "Give me segregation or give me death," one Alabama legislator proclaimed. But it was the black man who more often was faced with the choice.

The first great test of will between the segregationists and the federal government (which is charged with enforcing federal court orders) was acted out in Little Rock, Arkansas, in 1957. A city of the "New South," Little Rock was an unlikely stage for such a confrontation. It boasted a moderate mayor, an enlightened congressman, and a liberal newspaper, the Arkansas *Gazette*. Token integration had been accepted at the State University for years, and Little Rock had come up with a plan for integration that was actually little more than token. Finally, there was Governor Orval Faubus.

Born and reared in the Ozark Mountain country, Faubus had worked his way through high school and into politics. An expert woodsman, he also had been a fruit picker, teacher, newspaper editor and publisher, and an army officer during World War II. As governor, he had created a conservation commission, relaxed welfare provisions, encouraged industrial development, and declared that the "problem" of school integration "should be solved on the local community level."

So his decision to send National Guardsmen to prevent the integration of nine black students into Little Rock's Central High School surprised most observers. It "would not be possible to restore or maintain order if forcible integration is carried out tomorrow," Faubus explained in a television address on the eve of integration. When one of the nine students attempted to enter the school, she was turned back by a Guardsman. The crowd on hand cheered lustily and shouted insults at the girl as she left the scene.

In Washington, Dwight D. Eisenhower, the first Republican president in 20 years, was asked to comment on the incident. "You cannot change people's hearts merely by laws," he replied, a sentiment he had expressed in the past. Nevertheless, he dispatched agents of the Federal Bureau of Investigation to look into the matter.

Eisenhower, war hero and father figure to the American public, was in his second term of office. His presidency had been inactive; indeed, his critics saw him as a political innocent, a simple man who preferred golf, bridge and westerns to the exercise of power. But he was neither innocent nor simple. "Dwight Eisenhower," political analyst Murray Kempton wrote some years later, "was as indifferent as Calvin Coolidge, as absolute as Abraham Lincoln, more contained than John Kennedy, more serpentine than Lyndon Johnson, as hard to work for as Andrew Johnson."

That he initiated no social reforms was not surprising. He had spent his career in the army and his time between the army and the presidency in the company of wealthy businessmen, environments not known for the development of social consciousness. Duty, however, he understood well. When Faubus complained about the "unwarranted interference" of the FBI agents, Eisenhower replied: "The only assurance I can give you is that the federal Constitution will be upheld by me by every legal means at my command."

The government obtained a court injunction preventing Governor Faubus from interfering with the integration of Central High School. When the black students returned, they were greeted by an ugly, belligerent mob straining against the state and local police barricades; the National Guard was absent. The students entered the school, but the mob grew so explosive that the students were removed from the school at noon for their own protection. Asked if they wanted to come back again, they replied that they would, "if we can come here without causing any trouble. The students will accept us once we go with them for a while."

That evening President Eisenhower denounced the "disgraceful occurrence" at Central High School. A federal court's orders, he said, "cannot be flouted with impunity by any individual or mob of extremists." He issued a proclamation ordering the mob to disperse. When the mob ignored the order, Eisenhower flew 1,000 paratroopers to Little Rock and federalized 10,000 members of the Arkansas National Guard to handle the situation. It was the first time since reconstruction that federal troops had been sent to the South to protect the rights of black people.

Under the protection of the troops, who patrolled the school for the rest of the academic year, the nine black students were integrated into Central High School. The segregationists took their further objections to court and lost. Governor Faubus then closed all of Little Rock's high schools for a term; but the law under which he acted was declared unconstitutional, and integration in Little Rock gradually was accepted.

The students themselves—white and black—expressed their attitudes in a remarkable interview with a Norwegian correspondent conducted for the National Broadcasting Company after the first day of integration. Four white students, three of them girls, were asked to discuss the situation with two of the black students, a boy and a girl. The correspondent asked the white students if they ever really had made an effort to find out what black people were like.

"Not until today," two of the girls replied.

"And what do you think about it after today?"

"Well," said one girl, "you know that my parents and a lot of the other students and their parents think that the Negroes aren't equal to us. But—I don't know. It seems like they are, to me."

One of the black students suggested that if the people of Little Rock would "get together" and try to discuss their different views, they might see integration differently.

"I know now," one of the girls volunteered, "that it isn't as bad as I thought it was—after we got together and discussed it."

Her friend added: "We both came down here today with our minds set . . . that we were fully against integration. But I know now that we're going to change our minds."

"What will your parents say to that?" the interviewer asked.

"I think I'm going to have a long talk with my parents," the girl replied.

Still, school integration proceeded slowly. And two years later, a new champion of segregation, Governor George C. Wallace of Alabama, stood in the doorway of the University of Alabama to bar the registration of two black students whom the federal district court had ordered enrolled.

Wallace was more pugnacious and more ambitious than Faubus, and at 44 years old, younger than Faubus. Known as "Little George," he had been an amateur bantamweight boxing champion in high school and had boxed professionally to help pay his way through law school. After four years in the army air force, he had plunged into Alabama politics, serving in the state legislature and as a circuit judge. As a legislator he had sponsored a number of measures beneficial to workers, and as a judge he had defied the U. S. Civil Rights Commission by refusing to turn over voter registration records. His governorship had been based on the same combination—economic aid to the working class and in his words, "segregation now, segregation tomorrow, segregation forever."

Wallace's doorway defiance was more symbolic than real; when President John F. Kennedy federalized part of the Alabama National Guard and sent it to the university, the Governor stepped aside. Later in 1963, Wallace again went through the motions. Several schools in Birmingham, Tuskegee and Mobile were scheduled to be integrated. Wallace first closed the schools in Birmingham, "to preserve the peace," then ordered National Guardsmen to bar the entrance of the black students. President Kennedy again federalized the Guardsmen and sent them back to their armories, and the schools finally were integrated.

But Wallace's defiance left its mark. In its wake came renewed violence in Alabama, in New York, in California, in Mississippi. Black churches were bombed, civil rights leaders and workers were assassinated. As the Atlanta *Constitution* noted: "Irrational abuse and preachments of defiance of due process by persons in public life constitute a tree which bears . . . bitter fruits. . . ."

Such defiance also encouraged the use of various legal delaying tactics, and on the whole these were very effective.

112 *From Reconstruction to Revolution*

In 1965—eleven years after the *Brown* decision—the entire South had integrated only about 1 percent of its black students. Mississippi had not integrated a single student. The schools in Prince Edward County in Virginia had been closed since 1959. White children there attended a "private" school supported by public funds; black children stayed home. Finally, in 1964, the Supreme Court ordered Prince Edward County to reopen its schools. Speaking for the Court, Justice Hugo L. Black declared that the situation reflected "entirely too much deliberation and not enough speed."

The situation in the cities of the North and West was not much better. While no laws compelled formal, *de jure* school segregation as in the South, residential segregation created informal, *de facto* segregation in neighborhood schools. It was not the law, but it was real.

The NAACP challenged such a situation in court in New Rochelle, New York, in 1961. Black pupils were restricted by school districting to the Lincoln Elementary School, which was 100 percent black. The NAACP argued that it was just as unconstitutional to compel black children to attend a *de facto* segregated school in the North as a *de jure* segregated school in the South. New Rochelle claimed that Lincoln was simply a "neighborhood school" and that the neighborhood just happened to be black. But testimony at the trial revealed that in 1930 New Rochelle had "gerrymandered" the school district—redrawn its boundaries to match those of the black neighborhood.

The court did not rule on the *de facto* argument. Instead, it found that the gerrymandering had violated equal protection under the Fourteenth Amendment and ordered that the black children be given free access to other schools. Shortly afterward, New Rochelle closed the Lincoln School and bussed its pupils to balanced schools throughout the city.

Encouraged by the New Rochelle victory, black leaders attacked *de facto* school segregation in New York, Detroit, Pittsburgh, Buffalo, Boston, Philadelphia, Chicago, San Francisco and a host of other cities, large and small. A number of plans were developed to meet the challenges. Some school systems redrew their districts to integrate them more; many adopted open enrollment, allowing students to bus to any school; others mixed and matched nearby segregated schools. But all these were little more than stopgap measures, for the root of the problem lay in the segregated neighborhoods themselves, and little was done to integrate those.

That American schools must be integrated, no longer can be doubted by reasonable men. In a two year study of school desegregation, child psychologist Robert Coles found that in mixed classes even children from hard-core segregationist homes often began, "with increasing compassion and respect, to see [their black classmates] as individuals." And the 1966 Coleman Report concluded that integration was the single most effective instrument for improving the education of black children because it gave them access to better schools. "Integration alone," sociologist James Coleman, the principal author of the report, repeated recently, "reduces the existing gap between black and white children by 30 percent. All the other school factors don't add up to nearly that much."

Between 1964 and 1970, the percentage of integrated black students in the South increased from about one percent to about 35 percent. The principal reason was the 1964 Civil Rights Act, which prohibited racial discrimination in any institution receiving federal funds. In the nation's cities, however, *de facto* segregation became more entrenched—and more intolerable. Yet white Americans continued to mark time. One is reminded of Edmund Burke's remark in 1770. "The only thing necessary for the triumph of evil," the British statesman said in *Thoughts on the Cause of Present Discontent*, "is for good men to do nothing."

Although the educational gains of the *Brown* decision failed to live up to expectations, its repercussions spread far beyond its original scope.

Most of these effects were entirely unexpected. First, the decision awakened northern public opinion to the existence of racism. Since reconstruction, blacks had been "invisible" outside the South. "They were down South somewhere, or over on the other side of the city, buried," one northerner admitted.

The existence of racism was made more vivid by the violent reaction of some segregationists to school integration. Most Americans—North and South—were appalled by the bombings of black schools and churches. They were shocked by the sight on their television screens of white adults screaming, "Nigger! Nigger! Nigger! Nigger! Nigger!" at black school children. "The southern leaders overplayed their hand," legal expert Alexander M. Bickel observed. "Mob action led to the mobilization of northern opinion in support of the Court's decision—not merely because the mob [was] disorderly, but because it [personified] the abstraction of racism."

The decision also disproved the contention, stated in 1907 by sociologist William Graham Sumner and often cited by opponents of civil rights legislation, that "stateways"—that is, laws—"cannot change folkways." President Eisenhower's sentiment that "you cannot change people's hearts merely by laws" was the modern equivalent of Sumner's axiom. But less than 20 years after the decision, movie houses, restaurants, hotels, ballparks, buses and trains and their terminals, and most other public facilities were integrated in the South—a development that few southerners would have predicted in 1954. White southerners fiercely resisted every change in their racial folkways, but once the change had been proved irreversible, they accepted it.

Much of the impetus for change was brought about by a new militancy among the blacks which at first expressed itself in direct, nonviolent protest. Direct, nonviolent action by blacks dated back at least to Frederick Douglass, who purposely had ridden in the "white" coaches of segregated trains. His forcible eviction from one such train had led to the integration of railroad travel in Massachusetts many years before the Civil War. Later, during reconstruction, a black youth had insisted on sitting in a "white only" horsedrawn streetcar in Louisville, Kentucky. Dragged from the car by hostile white teenagers, he then had been arrested. But the next day other blacks had launched a sit-in in the streetcars. Silently, they had endured the abuse of outraged white passengers. Finally, the streetcar company had agreed to integrate its vehicles, admitting that "it was useless to try to resist . . . the claim of Negroes to ride in the cars."

That had been in 1871. Seventy-one years later, in 1942, two men, one black and one white, sat down in a prosperous coffee shop in Chicago and asked for a cup of coffee. The black man was refused service. An attempt to reason with the management failed. White customers, the management insisted, wouldn't eat beside black people. The men offered to reimburse the management for any loss in business if the coffee shop would serve blacks for a short trial period. Refusing the offer, the management instead put up a sign announcing: "We reserve the right to seat our patrons where we choose."

Shortly afterward, an integrated group of 21 men and women—students and business and professional people—walked into the coffee shop and sat together at the counter. The blacks were directed to the basement for service, but they replied that they wished to sit with their friends. Meanwhile, the whites refused to eat the food that was served to them unless their black friends also were served. The management called the police.

When the police arrived, they were asked to eject the group on the basis of the seating announcement. "There is nothing in the law that permits us to do that," the police explained and left. The management held out another hour, then served the entire group. The first organized sit-in of the Congress of Racial Equality had succeeded.

A new, interracial activist organization, CORE practiced the discipline and tactics of India's great nationalist leader, Mohandas Gandhi: relentless noncooperation, economic boycott, civil disobedience. The idea of using them in the civil rights struggle had come from James Farmer, a twenty-two-year-old pacifist and former divinity student. Farmer, a native of Texas, had grown up with a strong sense of racial justice and human brotherhood. His first job in Chicago had been with the Fellowship of Reconciliation, a largely white, pacifist organization. CORE had been formed from this group.

CORE lay dormant for many years while Farmer organized interracial locals of the upholsterers' union in the South and worked for the NAACP. When the next spontaneous sit-in occurred, this time by black students in Greensboro, North Carolina in February 1960, Farmer was National Program Director of the NAACP, assisting displaced black sharecroppers in Tennessee who had dared to register to vote. The new wave of sit-ins revitalized CORE, and in 1961, Farmer left his position with the NAACP to become CORE's first National Director. He held this job until 1965, when he resigned to launch a proposed project for the development of literacy and job skills among the chronically unemployed. But the funds he thought had been promised to him never materialized. He taught instead until 1969, when he became Assistant Secretary of the Department of Health, Education and Welfare.

By then, black activists had left Farmer behind. But in 1961, they were just catching up to him. The Greensboro sit-in was a hastily improvised action. A black student from the town's black college had been refused service at the lunch counter of the local bus station. Angered, he returned to the campus and discussed the incident with his friends. What could they do to stop this form of discrimination? They decided on a plan. The next day four students went to the local Woolworth's, bought some school supplies without incident, then sat down at the store's lunch counter and asked for a cup of coffee.

They were refused. But, instead of leaving, they continued to sit at the counter. "They can just sit there," the store manager said. "It's nothing to me."

The students remained on the stools until the store closed. They sat again the next day. And the next day after that. On the fourth day, they were joined by some white students. The sit-in continued. At the end of six months, the lunch counter was integrated.

Meanwhile, the idea spread rapidly. Within two weeks of the Greensboro action, sit-ins began in fifteen cities in five southern states. In the next twelve months, 50,000 people, most of them black, participated in some kind of direct action in 100 cities—sit-ins at lunch counters,

Sit-in at Greensboro, North Carolina, 1960. *United Press International Photo.* "They were kids my age, and I knew this had something to do with my own life."

stand-ins at movies, kneel-ins at churches, read-ins at libraries, wade-ins at beaches. They were insulted, beaten, gassed, even shot; 3,600 of them were jailed. But they prevailed.

The effect of the Greensboro sit-in was electrifying. Robert Parris Moses, a young New York schoolteacher, expressed the reaction of many young people to the situation. Moses had seen a picture of the sit-in in his newspaper. "The students in that picture," he said later, "had a certain look on their faces, sort of sullen, angry, determined. Before, the Negro in the South had always looked on the defensive, cringing. This time they were taking the initiative. They were kids my age, and I knew this had something to do with my own life."

From everywhere young people were drawn to the struggle. Julian Bond, a student in Atlanta whose interests were poetry and journalism, immediately began organizing his fellow students to sit-in in Atlanta. Five years later, he was elected to the Georgia legislature, and in 1968 he was nominated for the Vice-Presidential spot on the Democratic national ticket. Charles McDew, an athletic Ohio boy studying in South Carolina, helped to organize a local sit-in. A recent convert to Judaism, he had read in his Talmud: "If I am not for myself, then who is for me? If I am for myself alone, then what am I? If not now, when?" Greensboro had answered the questions.

The sudden wave of sit-ins took the established civil rights organizations by surprise. "The younger generation is challenging us to forget our laziness and doubt and fear and to follow our dedication to the truth to the bitter end," Ella Baker, a veteran civil rights organizer, told her friends in the established civil rights organizations. Neither the NAACP nor the Urban League had had experience with protest demonstrations in the South, and CORE, which was rich in experience, was a northern-based organization, with only a few staff members in the South. Support from all groups, however, followed quickly. CORE, in particular, sent staff members to Greensboro and other cities to instruct demonstrators in nonviolent techniques and discipline. This instruction included how to position the body to protect against head-cracking, face-disfigurement and internal injuries from kicks.

As the action spread southward, demonstrators found themselves increasingly in need of these instructions. In Nashville, Tennessee, white hecklers pressed lighted cigarettes against the backs of girls sitting at a counter and pulled other demonstrators off their stools and beat them (the police arrested the victims). In Atlanta, Georgia, acid was thrown at a sit-in leader. In Jacksonville, Florida, a student's jaw was broken in jail. In Biloxi, Mississippi, a white mob attacked blacks wading at a beach with guns, chains and clubs. In Houston, Texas, the local Klan kidnapped a black demonstrator, flogged him with a chain and carved "KKK" on his chest.

But the demonstrators kept sitting, standing, kneeling, marching—burrowing into the structure of southern segregation. Most of their actions violated either local or state laws. But the activists believed that many of these laws were unconstitutional and that, furthermore, they had been passed by legislatures chosen by an electorate from which blacks had been illegally excluded. Why, then, should blacks be bound by such laws? As one freedom song noted:

> *It isn't nice to block the doorway,*
> *It isn't nice to go to jail.*
> *There are nicer ways to do it,*
> *But the nice ways always fail.*

There also was the question of public vs. private rights. A restaurant was privately owned but publicly used. The black man was concerned only with the public aspect of private enterprise. He did not demand to be admitted to private *ownership*. But he did demand the right of public *use*.

The Supreme Court upheld the demonstrators in a series of key decisions beginning in 1961. That year, in *Garner*

v. *Louisiana,* the Court overturned a sit-in conviction that had been obtained on the basis of a "breach of the peace." It was no breach of the peace, said Chief Justice Earl Warren in the majority opinion, for the demonstrators to "sit peacefully in a place where custom decreed they should not sit."

In 1963 the Court reversed a number of convictions for sit-ins that had been based upon "criminal trespass." South Carolina's segregation ordinance, the Court decided in the leading case, *Peterson* v. *Greenville,* violated the equal protection clause of the Fourteenth Amendment. And, in 1964, the Court overturned another group of trespass convictions. The Constitution, said Justice Arthur Goldberg, in the leading case, *Bell* v. *Maryland,* "guarantees to all Americans the right to be treated as equal members of the community with respect to public accommodations."

Even southerners who deplored the demonstrators' goals were impressed by their discipline—and repelled by their hecklers. The Richmond *News Leader,* commenting on a sit-in in that city, observed:

> Here were the colored students, in coats, white shirts, ties, and one of them was reading Goethe and one was taking notes from a biology text. And here, on the sidewalk outside, was a gang of white boys come to heckle, a ragtail rabble, slack-jawed, black jacketed, grinning fit to kill. . . . Eheu! It gives one pause.

During 1960, CORE was kept busy organizing sit-ins. And after eighteen years of operating on a small scale, it began expanding rapidly. New branches were formed, staff workers were hired, volunteers came around looking for ways to help. In February, 1961, delegates from 100 branches convened in New York and unanimously elected Farmer their National Director.

CORE's emergence as a major national civil rights organization brought to four the number of such groups in the "Movement," as the thrust for equality is often called. The other three were the NAACP, the Urban League and the Southern Christian Leadership Conference (SCLC), which Martin Luther King, Jr. had helped organize in 1957. Meanwhile, the student activists, who were more radical in their thinking and less concerned with respectability than their elders, wanted to be independent. So, even as CORE expanded, SCLC helped to organize another group, the Student Nonviolent Coordinating Committee, which later became the fifth powerful civil rights organization.

Ella Baker, the executive secretary of SCLC's Atlanta office, was the catalyst, organizing a meeting of student leaders in Raleigh, North Carolina, in the spring of 1960. At the first meeting, 126 student delegates and their friends joined together to sing what was by then the anthem of the nonviolent revolution, "We Shall Overcome." One delegate later described the scene: "Students had just come in from all over the South, meeting for the first time. . . . There was no SNCC. . . . no committees, no funds, just people who did not know what to expect but who came and released the common vision in that song."

In October, SNCC became permanent. Sixteen young people, fifteen of them black, gave up their studies, their careers, to work full time in the South organizing activities. Charles McDew was elected chairman, and a headquarters was established in a windowless cubicle of the SCLC's Atlanta office. Declaring the foundation of its actions to be "the philosophical or religious ideal of nonviolence," SNCC began "coordinating." At first, with no funds, little experience and everyone busy demonstrating or serving jail sentences, there was a minimum of coordination. By the fall of 1961, however, SNCC was ready to funnel its energies into two basic activities: a continuation of direct action demonstrations and a drive to register black voters in the deep South.

The first voter registration schools opened in August in Mississippi, where as one observer noted, "the law is still the law as enforced by the sheriff, not the law that comes out of Washington." In Mississippi in 1961, 50 percent of the eligible white voters were registered, only 5 percent of the eligible black voters were. It was worse in some rural counties. Leflore County, for example, had approximately 50,000 people, about two-thirds of them black. Ninety-five percent of the eligible white voters were registered, only two percent of the eligible black voters were. In Haywood County, which was 61 percent black, not a single black person had voted since reconstruction!

Mississippi—fertile, poor, proud, backward, violent—was the last stronghold of the old Confederacy. To Mississippians, segregation was a way of life. And they were determined that nothing would change it. "Sure, I reckon it's all right for a nigger to vote if he wants to and it don't harm nothing," a white Mississippian told a reporter in 1961, "but what if they all begun to vote here! We'd be swamped. You put *yourself* in *our* place, and you'll see why we got to keep *them* in *their* place."

From his own, narrow point of view, that man was right. Within ten years, the blacks in his county, few of whom ever had voted before, had elected virtually an all-black slate of officials. Life in Mississippi never again would be the same.

But change came slowly. The first SNCC workers were kicked, clubbed, pistol-whipped and jailed; and two black farmers were shot to death. Only a few new voters were registered. In the spring of 1962, SNCC joined with the

NAACP, CORE and SCLC to form the Council of Federated Organizations (COFO) to coordinate voter registration programs in Mississippi. At the same time, the Voter Education Project was formed to help register black voters throughout the entire South. Financed by private foundations, the VEP was administered by the Southern Regional Council in Atlanta, an interracial organization that since 1944 had worked for racial justice.

With additional workers and resources, voter registration picked up—but so did the violence. SNCC offices were burned, SNCC workers were slugged, shot and arrested, and in jail they were beaten and tortured. Medgar Evers, the thirty-seven-year-old secretary of the NAACP in Mississippi, was assassinated in his driveway by a sniper.

No one was inviolate. Mrs. Fannie Lou Hamer, a forty-seven-year-old sharecropper with two children, attended a SNCC meeting, and the next day went down to register "because," she said later, "for one time I wanted things to be different." She was evicted immediately from the plantation where she had worked for eighteen years. Ten days later, sixteen bullets were pumped into her bedroom from a passing car. Fortunately, she was out. Several months later, Mrs. Hamer, by then a SNCC worker, was jailed on a trumped-up charge and beaten with a blackjack.

Still, the program continued. It was characteristic of SNCC workers that they did not come into a community, organize a demonstration, then move on and leave the local people to face the white reaction alone. They stayed on, living, working, suffering with the people they organized. This helped them gain the local blacks' confidence. "All these years," an aged black farmer told a SNCC meeting in 1963, "going along behind my plow, I thought some day things would change. But I never dreamed I'd see it now."

In 1964, COFO coordinated a "Summer Freedom Project" in Mississippi. Students and professionals—doctors, nurses, lawyers, teachers, ministers—more than 1,000 altogether, fanned out over the state to instruct, medicate and defend the blacks and register voters. About three-quarters of them were SNCC workers. More than 30 "Freedom Schools" sprung up where black children might get their first look into the worlds beyond the Mississippi backwaters. Describing one of the schools, a teacher said: "It was hard . . . the school was cramped, noisy. . . . We sat in a circle rather than the usual classroom format, to stress the equality of teacher and student. I read to them from Thomas Wolfe's *You Can't Go Home Again* and from Martin Luther King's *I Have a Dream,* then had them write speeches as if they were senators urging passage of the [1964] civil rights bill."

Once again, Mississippi was racked by violence. Thirty-five churches were burned, 30 homes and other buildings were bombed. Eighty people were beaten, three were shot, and three students—Michael Schwerner and Andrew Goodman of New York and James Chaney of Meridian—were murdered in cold blood.

The price was far too high, but the last stronghold of the old Confederacy had been breached. That summer, Mississippi blacks organized the Freedom Democratic Party. In the fall the FDP sent a delegation to the Democratic National Convention to claim those seats traditionally held by white Mississippians, who kept blacks out of the party machinery. President Lyndon Johnson, who was certain to be renominated and anxious to avoid an intra-party struggle, sought to arrange a compromise. Two FDP delegates would be added to the regular Mississippi delegation, and the rest of the FDP delegation would be seated on the convention floor as "honored guests." The FDP rejected the compromise and, lacking national support, ended up with no representation. But it made its presence felt when a sit-in it staged on the convention floor was picked up by national television, and it has remained a potent force in Mississippi politics.

In terms of voter registration, the gains of SNCC's drive were modest. By the end of 1964, about seven percent of the eligible black voters in Mississippi were registered, an increase of about two percent over 1961. In the South as a whole, the ratio was about 40 percent, up from about 25 percent in 1961. (By 1970, this ratio had increased to about 65 percent.)

The really significant gains lay in the *human* changes effected by the drive. For many blacks, it was an awakening. And, for many whites, it was a revelation, as indicated by the attitude expressed in the following exchange from the 1964 trial of Medgar Evers' accused assassin:

"Do you think it is a crime for a white man to kill a nigger in Mississippi?" the prosecuting attorney asked a prospective juror.

"What was his answer?" inquired the judge.

"He's thinking it over," the attorney replied.

That, in Mississippi, was progress.

While some SNCC workers concentrated on voter registration in the South, others continued to coordinate direct action demonstrations. After the spring of 1961, this mainly involved "freedom rides."

Actually, the freedom rides were a CORE creation. Along with the Fellowship of Reconciliation, CORE had sponsored the first ride in 1947 through the upper South. Called a "journey of reconciliation," it had been organized to test enforcement of the Supreme Court's 1946 ban on discrimination in interstate buses. Bayard Rustin, one of the organizers of the ride, had spent 30 days on a North Carolina chain gang as a result of it.

Fourteen years later, CORE's National Director, James Farmer, called for another ride, this one through the deep South to New Orleans. Farmer himself was the first volunteer; James Peck, a veteran white CORE staffer, was the second. Also among the seven black and six white riders was John Lewis, later chairman of SNCC. The ride began on May 4 in Washington, D.C. in two buses.

The proposed route snaked through the heart of the old Confederacy: Richmond, Lynchburg, Charlotte, Rock Hill, Augusta, Atlanta, Anniston, Birmingham, Montgomery, Meridian, Jackson, New Orleans. Through the rolling valleys of Virginia and the spring-green forests of North Carolina, the buses cruised without incident. In Rock Hill, South Carolina, a gang of thugs slugged two riders; but the buses continued to Atlanta without further trouble. Then, on Mother's Day, they moved into Alabama.

Outside of Anniston, a mob stopped the first bus, slashed its tires and hurled a fire bomb through a window. Choking from the smoke, the riders groped their way outside where they watched the bus burn to a charred steel skeleton.

Meanwhile, the second bus, an hour behind the first one, rolled into Birmingham, where another mob, armed with lead pipes and clubs, waited. As James Peck and Charles Person, an Atlanta sit-in demonstrator, stepped into the "white" waiting room, a dozen men dragged them into an alleyway and pummeled them with fists and pipes. Peck was beaten unconscious. Fifty-five stitches later were required to close his head wounds.

Through all this, the police, noted one report, "were either inactive, not present, or strangely late in arrival." When Birmingham's police chief, Eugene "Bull" Connor, was asked where the police had been, he replied that they were off for Mother's Day.

The next day, the riders regrouped in Birmingham, but no driver would take them to Montgomery. Finally, they gave up and flew out of the city to New Orleans, their destination.

At this point, a group of SNCC workers in Nashville and Atlanta decided to complete the ride to show that it could not be stopped by violence. They met in Birmingham, where a driver finally agreed to take them to Montgomery. The evening before the ride was to begin, Governor John Patterson assured one of President Kennedy's aides that Alabama would "fully protect everyone."

The bus moved out of Birmingham. At the Montgomery city limits, it was greeted by police cars and helicopters. But inside the city, the police escort disappeared and a welcoming mob at the bus terminal swung into action. Club-carrying youths pounded one rider to the pavement, then stomped his face into the hot tar. He got up, the youths smashed him down again. The President's aide, the same man who had relayed Governor Patterson's assurances to Washington, was himself struck unconscious.

The police finally arrived and broke up the mob, which had swelled to over 1,000. Ambulances were summoned for the wounded, but only one came, from a black hospital. "Every white ambulance in town reports their vehicles have broken down," Montgomery's police commissioner, L. B. Sullivan, explained to a reporter.

In Washington, Attorney General Robert F. Kennedy ordered 500 federal marshals into Montgomery. The next day, Governor Patterson called out the National Guard.

Several days later, the freedom riders left Montgomery for Jackson, Mississippi, where they were thrown in jail for "breach of the peace." More freedom riders followed them. They also were arrested. But still more came—not only to Jackson but to cities throughout the South.

Most of these cities reacted predictably. Those riders who were not assaulted were arrested on trumped-up charges. In fact, it was the local officials who were violating federal law; but the Justice Department made little effort to enforce the law.

This was true not only in relation to freedom rides but also in relation to voter registration and other activities. Civil rights workers' pleas for protection were repeatedly ignored by Washington. The workers, understandably, became skeptical of the Administration's commitment to racial equality.

Events in Georgia's "black belt" in the fall of 1961 revealed the scope of this problem. In this rich agricultural region, life had not changed much since the 1890's. "I picked cotton and pecans for two cents a pound," a sixteen-year-old boy from a large plantation explained. "I went to the fields at six in the morning and worked until seven in the afternoon. When it came time to weigh up, my heart, body and bones would be aching, burning and trembling. I stood there and looked the white men right in their eyes while they cheated me. . . ."

"We want our colored people to go on living like they have for the last 100 years," said Sheriff Zeke T. Matthews of Terrell County. Matthews had been in office 20 years without opposition—and no wonder. Although blacks outnumbered whites in Terrell County almost two to one, 2,894 whites were registered to vote, only 51 blacks were.

In October, 1961, SNCC workers moved into Albany,

Segregated theatre in Mississippi. *The New York Times.*

a tidy city of 57,000 people just outside Terrell County, to wake up the area's blacks to the 20th century. The workers began by organizing students, registering voters, turning out leaflets and teaching the techniques of nonviolence. In November, they rode a bus into Albany to test enforcement of a new Interstate Commerce Commission ruling against segregated terminals. When they walked into the "white" waiting room, they were evicted by police. The violation was reported to Washington, but no action was taken.

Three subsequent attempts to desegregate the terminal were met with arrests, which triggered mass demonstrations, sit-ins, further arrests, repression and, ultimately, police violence. Washington's response was token. "Through more than three years of conflict and pain in Albany," wrote Howard Zinn, a political scientist who also participated in many of the Albany events, "the national government failed again and again to defend the Constitutional rights of Negroes in that city." This was typical throughout the South. In the backwaters, white atrocities went unpunished—indeed, unnoticed. Local agents of the Federal Bureau of Investigation for the most part were uncooperative, sometimes hostile.

In the face of such government indifference and white brutality, black activists became increasingly restless, increasingly skeptical of the effectiveness of nonviolence. "Very few of us accept nonviolence as a way of life," a SNCC worker in violence-ridden Mississippi admitted. "We were willing to accept it as long as it was sanity, but it's just not sanity to give your life away."

"History is the long and tragic story of the fact that privileged groups seldom give up their privileges voluntarily."

Martin Luther King, Jr.

THE TWILIGHT OF NONVIOLENCE

When Martin Luther King, Jr., the apostle of nonviolence, organized and became head of the Southern Christian Leadership Conference, he was probably the most influential black leader since Booker T. Washington. In the eyes of some black militants, in fact, the comparison is more than appropriate. They see King as misguided, naive, opportunistic, even Uncle Tomish—a far cry from the popular image of him as a martyred hero. That is a minority opinion, of course, and as exaggerated as the image of the hero. But many who might dispute the militants' assessments still would agree with radical poet and writer Julius Lester, who concluded that King was "not a leader, but a symbol."

It is perhaps a fitting irony that King, a very human man with human strengths and weaknesses, should be in life a symbol and in death a martyr. He once said that history had thrust him into his position in the civil rights movement, and that was true. But once the mantle was placed on his shoulders, he knew what to do with it. Indeed, admitted E. D. Nixon, the organizer who drew King into the Montgomery bus boycott in 1955, the boycott committee was just looking for an agreeable figurehead—"and we got a Moses."

Until then, King's life was uneventful. Born in 1929 in Atlanta, he was christened Michael Luther, after his father, the Rev. Michael Luther King, Sr. His father later changed both their names to Martin Luther, in honor of the great Protestant reformer. As a boy, Martin, Jr. was called M.L. He was an aggressive competitor in sports. Despite his shortness, he played fullback in football "because he ran over anybody who got in his way."

Always a careful dresser, King was known as "Tweed" in his youth for his fondness for fashion. He also was a ladies' man. "He had his share of girlfriends, and I decided I couldn't keep up with him," admitted his younger brother. "Especially since he was crazy about dances and just about the best jitterbug in town." *

At dances, King often was the "enforcer," the strong man who kept order. In later years he maintained that he "never liked to fight," even when provoked. His boyhood friends recall that he seldom had to. In a showdown, his standard challenge was to a no-holds-barred wrestling match—"Let's go to the grass." According to an old acquaintance, if King saw someone "dancing too close to a girl or giving her a hard time . . . he'd come over and try to joke you out of it. If you kept it up, he'd tell you flatly to stop it. And if you still kept on, you could expect: 'Let's go to the grass.'" Few took up the challenge.

Discussing King's well-known philosophy of passive resistance, the same man quipped: "The rest of the world is wondering how he got that way so young, and we all wonder how he got that way so quick."

The first knowledge of segregation came to King when he was five years old. His best friends, two white children, suddenly were forbidden by their parents to play with him. The parents, King recalled later, "weren't hostile; they just made excuses. Finally, I asked my mother about it." She explained why, then reassured him: "You are as good as anyone."

Further reminders of segregation inevitably followed—in school, in buses, in the movies, even in stores. When King was still a child, his father took him downtown to buy shoes. They sat down in the first empty seats at the front of the store. A white clerk approached them and said politely: "I'll be happy to wait on you if you'll just move to those seats in the rear."

The elder King replied: "There's nothing wrong with these seats. We're quite comfortable here."

"Sorry," said the clerk, "but you'll have to move."

"We'll either buy shoes sitting here," King's father said, "or we won't buy shoes at all." And, with that, father and son walked out.

The gesture was in keeping with the principles of the elder King. A power in the local NAACP, he had been active in several civil rights struggles in Atlanta. And for years he had refused to ride the city buses because blacks were treated so badly on them. At home, his word was law. He taught his children the solid middle-class virtues: respect, hard work, honesty, thrift, order, courtesy. Education, he told them, was the key to a useful life, religion was the key to a moral one. The day began and ended with family prayer, and at meals, M.L., his older sister, and his younger brother recited Bible verses they had memorized.

Bright and serious, King was a voracious reader always

looking to get himself "some big words." He skipped two grades in high school and entered Morehouse College at age fifteen. There, he was a joiner—the NAACP, the Young Men's Christian Association, the glee club, the student–faculty discipline committee—and a talker, not only in committees but in oratorical contests as well. During summer vacations, he worked unloading trains and trucks.

King began college with thoughts of becoming a lawyer, or perhaps a doctor. The ministry did not appeal to him; ironically, he was put off by the "emotionalism" in the black church! But in his junior year he was persuaded by the president of Morehouse that religion "could be intellectually respectable as well as emotionally satisfying." He decided to study for the ministry, and a year later he was ordained in his father's church. In 1948, he was graduated from Morehouse.

That fall, he went to his first integrated school, Crozer Theological Seminary in Chester, Pennsylvania. There, among tree-shaded walks and manicured lawns, he studied and read: church management, sermonizing, the Christian philosophers, the Prophets, the Gospels, John Locke, Jean Jacques Rousseau, Adam Smith, Karl Marx, Mohandas Gandhi. All but the first (King never became a good administrator) left their imprint upon him. He later said: "From my Christian background I gained my ideals and from Gandhi my operational technique."

After leaving Crozer, where he won top honors, King went to Boston College in 1951 on a fellowship to do graduate work. In Boston, he met Coretta Scott, beautiful, talented, bright, a graduate student at the New England Conservatory of Music. Driving her home from their first date, King told her, "You know, you have everything I ever wanted in a woman. We ought to get married some day." Less than two years later, in June 1953, they were married.

King already was receiving job offers from schools and churches, North and South. He accepted the pastorate of the Dexter Avenue Baptist Church in Montgomery, Alabama. Later, he explained that he had returned to the South, "in spite of the disadvantages," because he and his wife "had the feeling that something remarkable was unfolding in the South, and we wanted to be on hand to witness it." In September 1954, his work at Boston College finished, King began his first full-time pastorate. He was 25 years old. A little more than a year later, history took him over.

Montgomery, Alabama, the "Cradle of the Confederacy," in 1955 still slumbered in that southern dream world where white gentility was served obediently by respectful, contented blacks. The city was almost completely segregated. The main contact between the two races was that of white employers with their black domestics. Over life in Montgomery lay a veneer of white complacency, and under that, a current of rising black frustration.

That was the situation when, on a warm December day, Mrs. Rosa Parks, stepped onto a city bus in downtown Montgomery. Mrs. Parks, a dignified forty-three-year-old seamstress and former secretary of the local NAACP, had been on her feet all day. Tired, she took a seat in the first row of the "black" section. A few stops later, the bus filled up and the driver asked her to give up her seat to a white man who just had boarded. It was a common request, which usually was complied with, but Mrs. Parks refused to move. The driver summoned the police, and when they came for her, Mrs. Parks quietly asked: "Why do you push us around?"

"I don't know," replied one officer, "but the law is the law, and you're under arrest."

The news of Mrs. Parks' arrest quickly spread through the black community. Some indignant women called E. D. Nixon and suggested protesting the arrest with a black boycott of buses. He agreed and began calling various ministers and other black leaders to discuss the idea. The leaders, who seldom agreed on anything, agreed to meet the following evening in the Dexter Avenue Baptist Church, which had been offered by its pastor, the Rev. Martin Luther King, Jr.

That evening, a Friday, the leaders called for a one-day boycott on Monday and a community mass meeting for Monday evening to determine what to do next. Leaflets were mimeographed asking people not to "ride the buses to work, to town, to school, or anywhere on Monday." The black taxi companies agreed to carry passengers at bus rates. "If you work," the leaflets suggested, "take a cab, or share a ride, or walk."

One of these leaflets fell into the hands of a white housewife, who promptly passed it on to the Montgomery *Advertiser*. The newspaper printed it on the front page, with a critical story, and by Sunday afternoon almost all of Montgomery's 60,000, or so, blacks had heard of the boycott. "They gave us publicity we couldn't have bought," E.D. Nixon said later.

Then the police commissioner went on television and promised "protection" to any blacks who continued to ride the buses—another unwitting blunder.

"I knew our people, and I thought 60 percent of them would join the boycott," E.D. Nixon later explained. "Then this fellow put a motorcycle cop behind every bus, and the neutral Negroes saw that and figured there'd be trouble and stayed off. That way, he gave us 100 percent."

In the planning stage, however, nobody was sure how effective the boycott might be. King himself had doubts not only about its prospective effectiveness but also about its propriety. The *Advertiser*'s story had compared the bus boycott to the tactics of the White Citizens' Councils —the closing of public schools to avoid integration, economic reprisals against integrationists, intimidation of blacks, and so on. Was the whole idea unethical, King asked himself?

He conceded that the boycott could be used for unethical ends, and that in fact the White Citizens' Council used boycotts that way. But he decided that the bus boycott was different, that it would promote justice rather than perpetuate injustice, as the Council's actions did. Henry David Thoreau's *Essay on Civil Disobedience,* which King had read in college, came to mind. Thoreau in 1847, rather than pay his taxes, had gone to jail to protest the evil of slavery. The parallel was clear: "We were simply saying to the white community," King concluded, " 'We can no longer lend our cooperation to an evil system.' "

To accept evil without protesting against it was to cooperate with it, he decided. The only course for a man of conscience was to refuse to cooperate with the evil. This, he felt, was the nature of the boycotter's action. "From this moment," he later wrote, "I conceived of our movement as an act of massive noncooperation. From then on I rarely used the word 'boycott.' "

Monday came, and with it, uncertainty. Unable to sleep, the Kings arose at 5:30. The bus route with the heaviest concentration of black passengers passed right in front of their parlor window. They watched anxiously for the first bus, which was scheduled to pass at about six. King was in the kitchen when his wife cried: "Martin, Martin, come quickly!" He rushed to the window, she pointed joyfully at a slowly moving bus. It was empty. Normally it would have been full of domestics riding to work. The Kings waited for the next bus—also empty. Fifteen minutes later, a third bus passed. Only two white passengers were on it.

All over the city, the results were the same. Students, workers, children, old people shared rides or walked to their destination and back. The boycott was almost 100 percent effective.

That same morning, Mrs. Parks was convicted and fined $14.00 for violating the city's segregation law. She appealed the case. In the afternoon, the boycott leaders met and created a formal organization, the Montgomery Improvement Association (MIA). King was elected President, partly because he had not been in Montgomery long enough to incur the enmity of any of the other leaders, who were at loggerheads.

Unsure of whether or not to continue the boycott, the MIA leaders decided to be guided by the turnout and the spirit at the evening mass meeting. These proved to be exceptional. Several thousand people, unable to get into the church where the meeting was scheduled, milled on the street outside, creating a traffic jam. Their enthusiasm, recalled King, "swept everything along like an onrushing tidal wave."

King was scheduled to make the main address. After a rousing hymn, a prayer and a reading of Scripture, he rose to the pulpit. The red eyes of network television cameras blinked on, the crowd in the pews settled back to listen.

Speaking without notes, King reviewed the events that

had led to the boycott—Mrs. Parks' arrest, the long history of abuse and insult, even murder, of blacks on the city's buses. They had endured it all, he noted. "But there comes a time," he said in measured intensity, "when people get tired. We are here this evening to say to those who have mistreated us so long that we are tired—tired of being segregated and humiliated; tired of being kicked about by the brutal feet of oppression. . . ." Applause broke out, not only inside the church but also on the street, where the address was being carried by loudspeakers. King continued:

"For many years we have shown amazing patience. We have sometimes given our white brothers the feeling that we liked the way we were being treated. But we come here tonight to be saved from that patience that makes us patient with anything less than freedom and justice." More applause. His eloquence had won them; now he spelled out a course of action. It would be nonviolent.

"Our method will be that of persuasion, not coercion. We will only say to the people: 'Let your conscience be your guide.'" Quoting Jesus, he said: "Love your enemies, bless them that curse you, and pray for them that despitefully use you." Then he concluded:

"If you will protest courageously, and yet with dignity and Christian love, when the history books are written in future generations, the historians will have to pause and say: 'There lived a great people—a black people—who injected new meaning and dignity into the veins of civilization.' This is our challenge and our responsibility."

As King returned to his seat, the crowd gave him a standing ovation. The boycott was on.

It continued for more than a year, despite all efforts, legal and otherwise, to crush it. The city invoked a law requiring taxis to charge minimum fares higher than bus fares; the MIA, with the help of organizer Bayard Rustin, promptly put together a car pool that functioned, as the opposition admitted, "with military precision." King was arrested and jailed, but the incident merely strengthened his leadership. The city, in a "get tough" move, harassed black drivers and made mass arrests of black leaders; but this action only increased sympathy—and financial aid—for the movement from the rest of the nation. Anonymous callers constantly threatened King, and white extremists bombed his and other leaders' homes; still, nobody backed down. Most important, however, the people continued to walk rather than ride. One elderly woman, when asked if she was tired after several weeks of walking, replied: "My feets is tired, but my soul is at rest."

From the beginning, the MIA attempted to negotiate with the city. The blacks asked for first come, first served seating arrangements, with blacks loading from the back and whites from the front—a practice that already was in effect in such southern cities as Nashville, Atlanta and Mobile. They also asked for courteous treatment from the drivers and for the hiring—or at least the taking of applications—of blacks to drive those buses that served the predominantly black neighborhoods. All but the request for courtesy were rejected by the city.

Finally, the MIA challenged the local segregation law in federal court. The law was declared unconstitutional in a two to one decision. Montgomery appealed to the Supreme Court, which upheld the decision, and the buses were desegregated. The boycott ended, having cost the bus company $750,000.

After the blacks returned to the buses, violence again erupted—bullets were fired into loaded buses, and homes and churches were bombed—but it soon subsided, and whites and blacks rode Montgomery's buses together. "The skies," King later noted drily, "did not fall. . . ."

Throughout the long struggle, King preached the beauty and effectiveness of nonviolence, which he called "the ultimate form of persuasion." At regular biweekly (later weekly) meetings, which were rotated throughout Montgomery, he described what he called five important characteristics of nonviolent resistance.

First, he said, it is not a method for cowards; it is "passive physically, but strongly active spiritually . . . nonaggressive physically, but dynamically aggressive spiritually."

Second, it "does not seek to defeat or humiliate the opponent, but to win his friendship and understanding."

Third, its attack is directed "against forces of evil rather than against persons who happen to be doing that evil." The tension in Montgomery, he added, is not between white people and black people but between "justice and injustice."

Fourth, nonviolence requires a "willingness to accept suffering without retaliation, to accept blows from the opponent without striking back." He quoted Gandhi: "Rivers of blood may have to flow before we gain our freedom, but it must be our blood." If it was necessary to go to jail, he added, one should enter the cell, in Gandhi's words, "as a bridegroom enters the bride's chamber." Suffering redeems the sufferer, he explained—and also changes his tormentors. As Gandhi said: suffering is infinitely more powerful than the law of the jungle for converting the opponent and opening his ears, which are otherwise shut to the voice of reason."

Fifth, nonviolent resistance "avoids not only external physical violence but also internal violence of spirit. The nonviolent resister not only refuses to shoot his opponent but he also refuses to hate him. At the center of nonviolence stands the principle of love."

Love, in this connection, King explained, "means understanding, redemptive good will"—what in the Greek New Testament is called *agape.*

Agape is the glue of what King called "the beloved community." Unlike the other Greek words for love—*eros,* the yearning for the divine, and *philia,* an intimate affection between friends—*agape* signifies an attempt to "preserve and create community." With *agape,* one rises "to the position of loving the person who does the evil deed while hating the deed he does."

The Montgomery boycott made King a national figure; victory brought him honors and new responsibilities. In 1957, Bayard Rustin, who had assisted King throughout the Montgomery struggle, helped him organize the Southern Christian Leadership Conference. King was elected its first president.

SCLC, asking black people "to assert their human dignity by refusing further cooperation with evil," coordinated a series of bus boycotts in Atlanta, Tallahassee and other southern cities. These were successful, but attempts to secure the moral and tactical support of the Eisenhower Administration in further assaults upon segregation failed. Unable to move forward at home, King paid ceremonial visits to Africa and India. And, in 1958, he was almost killed in a Harlem department store by a forty-two-year-old black woman who plunged a letter opener into his chest while he was autographing copies of his first book. The woman, babbling hysterically that King was a "Communist," later was declared criminally insane.

The next year, King resigned his Montgomery pastorate to devote more time to SCLS, and in January 1960 he moved to Atlanta where he joined his father's church as assistant pastor. A month later, the sit-ins began in Greensboro. King helped organize SNCC; then the three activist groups of the movement—SCLC, SNCC and CORE—together utilized nonviolent techniques in sit-ins, freedom rides and voter registration drives.

As the white response became more violent, however, and as the violence showed no sign of stopping or of being stopped, many blacks became disenchanted with King's notion of nonviolence. They saw that pressure, not love, opened public facilities to blacks; that the white man's purse could be touched more effectively than his conscience; that suffering, rather than redeeming the sufferer, too often killed him. And they discovered what historian Howard Zinn has called "that large middle ground between pure force and pure moral appeal." It was an area that included self-defense in the face of danger. Blacks, in the movement and out, began to adjust to it.

King, of course, kept on a pure nonviolent course. "We will match your [the white man's] capacity to inflict suffering with our capacity to endure suffering," he insisted, paraphrasing Gandhi. "We will meet your physical force with soul force. Do what you will to us," he declared, "and we will still love you. . . . But we will soon wear you down by our capacity to suffer. And in winning our freedom, we will so appeal to your heart and conscience that we will win you in the process."

In the spring of 1963, he went to Birmingham, Alabama to prove it.

Birmingham in 1963 was as segregated as Montgomery had been in 1955, but not nearly so genteel. A product of America's post-Civil War industrial and commercial boom,

Birmingham was raw and tough, like the steel from its roaring mills. There was, said reporter James Reston, "something in the history and atmosphere of this place, some relationship between the idea of the supremacy of the dollar and the supremacy of the white man," that made the city's white leadership balk at integration.

Actually, Birmingham already was under siege. The Rev. Fred Lee Shuttlesworth, a courageous forty-one-year-old Baptist minister, had been agitating for his people's "human" rights since 1956. But the city, with its rabidly segregationist police commissioner, Eugene "Bull" Connor, had refused to grant blacks even token concessions. Then, in April 1963, Connor lost a runoff election for mayor to a slightly less rabid segregationist, Albert Boutwell. The white leadership insisted that a new day had dawned for Birmingham. Connor insisted that he could not be removed from office until 1965 and he went to court. Fred Shuttlesworth insisted it didn't make any difference; Boutwell, he said, was "just a dignified Bull Connor." The campaign began.

It was launched with sit-ins at the downtown stores' segregated lunch counters. The demonstrators were arrested. A modest march on city hall followed. The marchers were arrested. King, his close aide, Rev. Ralph Abernathy of Montgomery, and Fred Shuttlesworth, defying a court order against further demonstrations, led the next march. They were arrested and imprisoned.

While King was in jail, eight white Alabama clergymen published an open letter criticizing the demonstrations as "unwise and untimely" and calling for the observance of "law and order and common sense." In his reply, "Letter from Birmingham City Jail," King was more blunt and uncompromising than ever before or after.

Justifying the demonstrations, he wrote: "History is the

Birmingham, 1963. Photograph by Bob Adelman. "We will match your capacity to inflict suffering with our capacity to endure suffering." Martin Luther King, Jr.

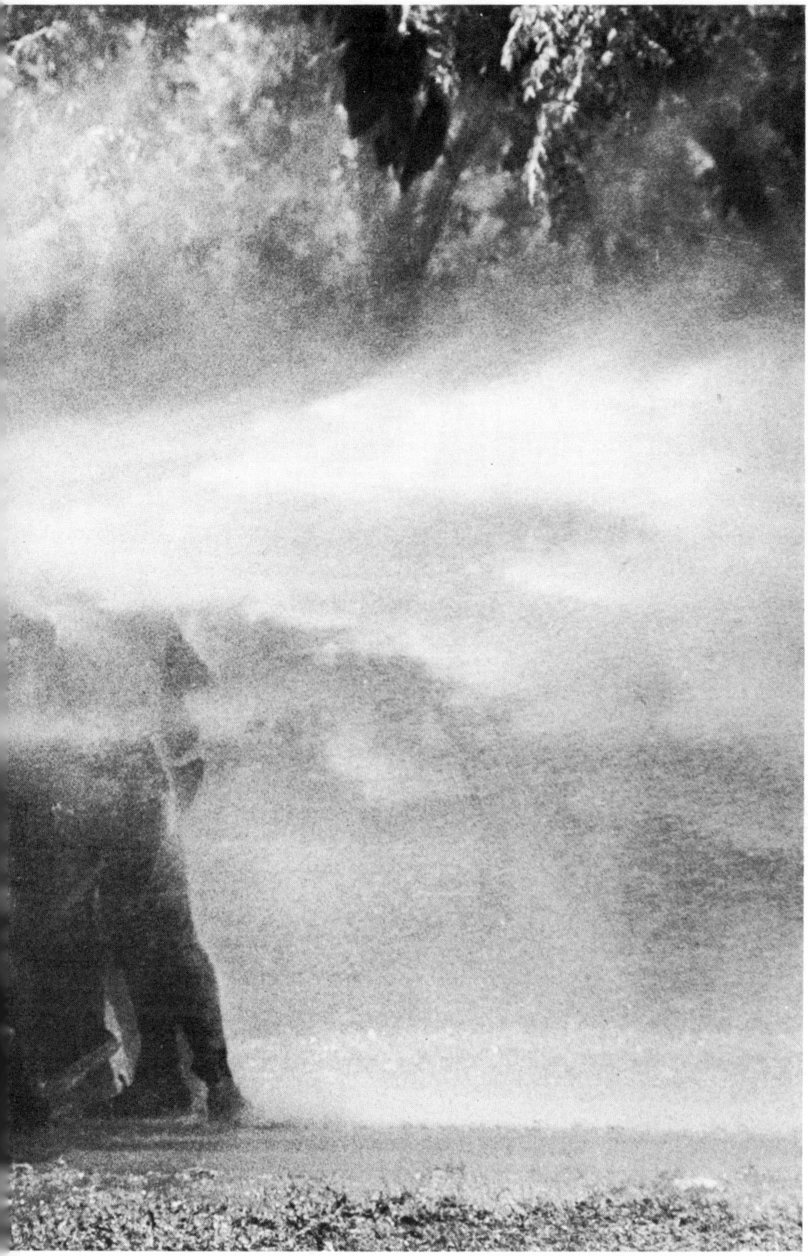

long and tragic story of the fact that privileged groups seldom give up their privileges voluntarily. Individuals may see the moral light and voluntarily give up their unjust posture; but . . . groups are more immoral than individuals."

On the breaking of laws, he cited Saint Augustine: "An unjust law is no law at all." And he defined an unjust law as "a code that a majority inflicts on a minority that is not binding on itself."

He was coming to the regrettable conclusion, he added, that the real stumbling block to equal rights was not "the Ku Klux Klanner but the white moderate who is more devoted to 'order' than to 'justice' . . . who paternalistically feels that he can set the timetable for another man's freedom. . . ."

Too many people, he explained, seemed to believe in "the strangely irrational notion that there is something in the very flow of time that will inevitably cure all ills. Actually time is neutral," he pointed out; and people of ill will appear to have used it better than have people of good will. This generation, he concluded, would have to repent "not merely for the vitriolic words and actions of the bad people but for the appalling silence of the good people."

Even so, he predicted, the black man would gain his freedom. "If the inexpressible cruelties of slavery could not stop us, the opposition we now face will surely fail."

After eight days in jail, King, Abernathy and Shuttlesworth were released on bond. The demonstrations continued, at least one each day, and so did the mass arrests. "I got plenty of room in the jails," Connor boasted. But the business community began to worry. As planned, the protesters were boycotting the segregated downtown stores, and the merchants were feeling the pinch. A few days after

Easter, fewer than 20 blacks—of a population of 150,000—were shopping in the downtown stores.

For 40 days in April and May, demonstrators marched or sat-in or knelt-in to protest segregation in Birmingham. More than 3,300 demonstrators were arrested, many of them school children. Connor loosed police dogs and high-pressure fire hoses on the demonstrators, then his men moved in with clubs to disperse them. Several students were bitten, then beaten; many others were flattened by jet blasts of water powerful enough to rip the bark off a tree. Fred Shuttlesworth was hurled against the side of a building by one such blast; as the prostrate minister was carried to an ambulance, Connor muttered, "I wish he'd been carried away in a hearse."

Americans everywhere were shocked when they saw these scenes on their television screens. So was President John F. Kennedy, whose narrow margin of victory in 1960 had been provided by black voters. Kennedy sent Assistant Attorney General Burke Marshall to Birmingham to see what he could do.

Marshall opened up lines of communication between the black leadership and the business community, and after several days of negotiating, a settlement was reached. The blacks' demands for the desegregation of lunch counters, rest rooms and drinking fountains and for the hiring and upgrading of blacks in white collar jobs were granted and a biracial committee was established. But instead of committing itself to negotiating further desegregation in Birmingham, as the blacks had demanded, the committee was designated merely as a "channel of communications" between the races.

The agreement, however, did not end the violence. One day after the accord, the front of the house of King's younger brother, the Rev. A. D. King, was demolished by a bomb. Another bomb rocked King's motel. Fortunately, no one was hurt. But in the melee that followed, angry black crowds clashed with police, stores and cars were burned and shattered. Calm was restored only after President Kennedy threatened to move in the National Guard. A few days later, the Alabama Supreme Court ruled Bull Connor out of office, and an uneasy truce settled over Birmingham.

Elsewhere, the violence continued into the summer. In Selma, Alabama, a black minister active in a voter registration drive was clubbed to the pavement by white assailants who lured him from his car by pretending to need help. In Danville, Virginia, marchers were beaten and hosed by the police. In Jackson, Mississippi, Medgar Evers was shot to death.

On June 11, 1963, President Kennedy went before the nation on television. He reviewed recent events and asked whether "all Americans are to be afforded equal rights and equal opportunities." Americans, he said, faced "a moral crisis as a country and as a people." It was not enough to demonstrate; it was time "to act in Congress . . ."

Eight days later, Kennedy asked Congress for legislation that would prohibit discrimination in public facilities, in federally assisted programs, in employment and in labor unions. It was the broadest civil rights program since 1875.

For Kennedy, the action was something of a turnabout. Early in his administration he had denied the need for civil rights legislation, claiming that executive orders could do what was necessary. Indeed, the enforcement powers—to say nothing of the *moral* powers—of the presidency were vast; but he had used them sparingly. He had even appointed staunch segregationists to federal courts in the South. Birmingham, apparently, had turned him around.

To dramatize the black man's struggle for equality, the

five big civil rights groups called for a massive march on Washington in August. Bayard Rustin, who originally suggested the march, was named its organizer by A. Philip Randolph, by now the elder statesman of the black leaders.

Tall, elegant, urbane, Rustin has been called "the most articulate strategist of the drive for Negro equality." He was born in 1910 in West Chester, Pennsylvania, where he won honors both in the classroom and on the playing field. An accomplished musician, he later supported himself singing and playing professionally. This complemented his activities as a pacifist, a socialist, and even, briefly, a Communist, when the party was agitating for civil rights. During World War II, he served 28 months in prison as a conscientious objector.

His commitment to the civil rights and labor movements had drawn him to A. Philip Randolph, who became his idol and mentor. A brilliant organizer, Rustin had helped in the formation of both SCLC and SNCC. Now, as the organizer of the march, he brought together what one reporter called "the greatest assembly for a redress of grievances that this capital has ever seen."

Reliable estimates of the number of marchers ran from 200,000 to 250,000. The marchers came, from farms and towns and cities all over the country. Black, white, young, old, rich, poor, famous, humble, they walked and sang together and, finally, in the shadow of the Lincoln Memorial, they stood together and listened to songs and speeches. Around the world, millions more tuned in on radio and television.

"We are the advance guard of a massive moral revolution," A. Philip Randolph told the huge crowd.

James Farmer, in jail in Louisiana, sent a message that was read by CORE's militant chairman, Floyd B. McKissick: "We will not stop until the dogs stop biting us in the

South and the rats stop biting us in the North."

Gospel singer Mahalia Jackson sang a sorrowful spiritual, which moved many in the crowd to tears.

Then Martin Luther King stepped up to the microphone. Behind him loomed the massive statue of Lincoln. Before him the green of the mall was blotted out by the cheering crowd of marchers, some of whom were cooling their feet in the long reflecting pools. In the distance rose the Washington Monument, still bright in the late afternoon haze.

King began and a hush fell over the crowd. He spoke eloquently of the black man's "marvelous new militancy" and the white man's realization that his freedom was "inextricably bound to our freedom." He added: "We cannot be satisfied as long as the Negro in Mississippi cannot vote and the Negro in New York believes he has nothing for which to vote." Then, he urged the marchers to go back to their homes with hope.

"I say to you today, my friends, even though we face the difficulties of today and tomorrow, I still have a dream. It is a dream deeply rooted in the American dream.

"I have a dream . . ." he continued, pausing. A few in the crowd shouted: "Tell us!"

". . . that one day this nation will rise up and live out the true meaning of its creed: 'We hold these truths to be self-evident, that all men are created equal.'

"I have a dream . . ." the crowd roared now—"Yes, yes!"

". . . that one day on the red hills of Georgia, the sons of former slaves and the sons of former slave owners will be able to sit together at the table of brotherhood.

"I have a dream . . ." another roar, and more shouts.

". . . that my four children will one day live in a nation where they will not be judged by the color of their skin but by the content of their character.

"I have a dream . . ." a great roar.

". . . that one day every valley shall be exalted, every hill and mountain shall be made low, the rough places will be made plain, and the crooked places will be made straight, and the glory of the Lord shall be revealed and all flesh shall see it together.

"This is our hope," King added, and as he concluded with a refrain from a black spiritual, the crowd roared again and waved their signs and banners.

Kennedy's civil rights bill, however, languished in the pigeonholes of hostile committees in Congress. Then, in November 1963, the President was assassinated in Dallas, Texas, and the racial crisis passed on to his successor, Lyndon B. Johnson, only the second southerner since Andrew Johnson to hold the office of President.

Lyndon Johnson, in fact, was in background and temperament remarkably like his namesake. Both were shaped in states in which southern attitudes were tempered by frontier conditions. Both began life in rural poverty and retained as adults a distrust for what might be called the eastern cosmopolitan complex. Both were self-made men and never forgot it. Both married women who were instrumental in their success. Both served in the United States Senate. Both were expedient—and controversial—choices for Vice-President. And both became President as the result of assassination.

It is one of the ironies of history that Lyndon Johnson inherited, 100 years later, the same problem that had led to the impeachment of Andrew Johnson.

Lyndon Baines Johnson was born in 1908 near Johnson City, Texas and shaped by the hard, bleak surrounding hill country. As a young man, he drifted to California. Later, he worked on a road gang for two years before enrolling at Southwest Texas State Teachers' College in 1927. In college he worked, politicked and majored in history. Graduated in 1930, he taught for a year, then went to Washington as secretary to a wealthy congressman. There he came under the tutelage of two wily Texans, Speaker of the House Sam Rayburn and Vice-President John Nance Garner. In 1934, he married Claudia Alta Taylor, who was as astute as she was gracious.

With an instinct for power and the will to achieve it, Johnson moved ahead inexorably from Roosevelt appointee to U. S. Representative to U. S. Senator (by 87 disputed votes). In the Senate, his cloakroom talents came to full flower as Minority, then Majority, Leader. "He doesn't have the best mind on the Democratic side of the Senate," said his mentor, Senator Richard Russell of Georgia. "He isn't the best orator; he isn't the best parliamentarian. But he's the best combination of all those qualities."

In 1960, Johnson sought the Democratic nomination for President but had to settle for second place on the ticket. Kennedy, one of his former aides wrote recently, chose Johnson as his running mate to get him out of the Senate so the Texan could be replaced as Majority Leader by a more cooperative man. "I'm 43 years old, and I'm the healthiest candidate for President in the United States. . . ." Kennedy reportedly told his aide. "I'm not going to die in office. So the vice-presidency doesn't mean anything." But events in Dallas proved him wrong, and Johnson was propelled from the echo chamber of the vice-presidency to the oval office of the White House.

"Let us continue," Johnson told the American people, as he sought to carry on Kennedy's programs. Observers wondered how hard he would fight for the civil rights bill, which was likely to be killed by a Senate filibuster if it ever got out of committee. It was the kind of legislation Johnson had voted against in the House and had quashed quietly in the Senate. He had supported voting rights legislation in 1957 and in 1960, but only after weakening it enough to please the southern leadership.

Johnson probably never had been the militant segregationist he made himself out to be at election time in segregationist Texas; more likely, he was content to reflect the attitudes of his constituents. But his constituency was larger now, and he was shrewd enough to sense that civil rights had become a popular cause. So, in the spring of 1964, he used his influence to pry the Kennedy bill out of committee. Then, working behind the scenes, he helped shut off the southern filibuster against it in the Senate. It was the first time a civil rights filibuster had been broken. A few weeks later, on July 2nd, Johnson signed the 1964 Civil Rights Act into law.

In its final form, the Act protected voting rights and entitled all persons "to the full and equal enjoyment of the goods, services, facilities, privileges, advantages and accommodations of any place of public accommodation." This was an unwitting tribute to the radicals, who had passed nearly identical legislation almost 100 years before.

The Act further provided for desegregation of schools and prohibited discrimination in federally assisted programs and in employment. It also established an Equal Employment Opportunity Commission and a Community Relations Service to mediate racial disputes. All of this was long overdue, but welcome.

Both King and Johnson were lauded for their roles in the victory. King received the Nobel Peace Prize, the third black man to be so honored. And, in the fall, Johnson was elected President in his own right, crushing Republican Barry Goldwater in an electoral landslide. Shortly afterward in *Heart of Atlanta Motel* v. *United States,* the Su-

Integrated train New Orleans, 1955. Photograph by Robert Frank.

preme Court upheld the constitutionality of the Civil Rights Act. As 1965 began, the prospects for racial justice achieved through a nonviolent revolution looked more promising than ever. But for King, for Johnson, and for nonviolence, 1965 marked the beginning of the end.

In January, King moved into Selma, Alabama, which he had chosen as the site of a "massive march" to test the voter registration provisions of the 1964 Civil Rights Act.

Selma, a former slave market and military depot of the

THE TWILIGHT OF NONVIOLENCE

Confederacy, lay deep in Alabama's black belt. Once a lynching town, it still was comparatively untouched by the 20th century. Only about two percent of the eligible black voters in Dallas County, of which Selma is the seat, were registered. And the ratio was that high only because SNCC workers had been pushing voter registration in Selma for two years.

King employed the strategy that had succeeded in Birmingham; frequent, small demonstrations to dramatize the issue. Hundreds were arrested, including King. The demonstrations spread outward, and in February a black laborer in Marion, 25 miles from Selma, was killed by a state trooper. At the funeral, King announced that he would lead a mass march from Selma to Montgomery, 54 miles away.

"Such a march," declared Governor George Wallace, "cannot and will not be tolerated."

The march began on March 7th, a Sunday. It was halted almost immediately by blue-helmeted state troopers and a sheriff's posse, who ordered the marchers to turn around. When they refused to budge, the troopers and posse, some of them mounted, waded into the crowd with billy clubs, whips and tear gas. Once again, television and newspaper coverage of the melee aroused the nation to anger. Sympathetic demonstrations were held in New York, Chicago, Los Angeles and Washington. Meanwhile, the marchers sought a court injunction forbidding state and local police from interfering with the march. The court agreed to hear the case and issued an order restraining the marchers until the issue was decided.

Two days later, the marchers set out again anyway, this time led by King. Again they found their way blocked by police. But King, under pressure not to disobey the court's restraining order, had agreed not to challenge the roadblock. The marchers knelt and prayed, then turned back.

Many of the young SNCC workers, who for some time had been falling away from King, SCLC and nonviolence, felt betrayed.

That night, white thugs in Selma brutally beat three white marchers, young clergymen, and killed one. Public anger was rekindled and thousands of Americans from all over the country began converging on Selma to add their presence to the march. President Johnson called a joint session of Congress and, in a nationally televised, impassioned address, asked for additional voting rights legislation. "It is not just Negroes but all of us who must overcome the crippling legacy of bigotry and injustice," he declared. "And we *shall* overcome," he concluded solemnly.

Within a week, the court ruled in the marchers' favor, and the march began again, this time under the protection of federal troops. It proceeded without incident, but after it was concluded, a white woman riding with a black youth was shot dead by a gunman in a passing car. She was the third person to die in the Selma demonstrations.

In August, Congress passed the 1965 Voting Rights Act, and President Johnson signed it into law. Basically, the Act outlawed literacy tests and other discriminating devices in any state where they were in effect or in any state where less than 50 percent of eligible voters were registered. Johnson called it "a victory for the freedom of the American nation."

It was the last such victory. One week after the signing of the Voting Rights Act, Watts, the black ghetto of Los Angeles, exploded in rebellion. The revolt in the ghettos had started. And with it emerged the white "backlash"—resistance to the black man's further demands for equality on the supposition that he "had gone too far" and was being "coddled."

This resistance was nothing new, of course. White America's ingrained racism merely was resurfacing. As King later said: "White America was ready to demand that the Negro should be spared the lash of brutality and coarse degradation, but it had never been truly committed to helping him out of poverty, exploitation, or all forms of discrimination." Indeed, most whites, King added, proceeded "from a premise that equality is a loose expression for improvement." They sought not to close the racial gap but "only to make it less painful and less obvious."

The white backlash stimulated greater black militance. In the summer of 1966, there were ghetto uprisings in more than a dozen American cities. National Guard troops were summoned in Chicago, where King was leading demonstrations for open housing, and in Cleveland, Dayton, Milwaukee and San Francisco. One newspaper characterized the rioters as "black mobsters," and Congress, sensing which way the white wind was blowing, allowed a bill compelling open housing to die in a Senate filibuster.

"I think I made one mistake," King reportedly told a friend in private. "I underestimated the depths of hate in America."

Events moved rapidly. White supremacists and "law and order" candidates ran well all over the country in the fall. In January 1967, Harlem's Representative Adam Clayton Powell, with 24 years of seniority, was denied his seat by the house for "irregularities," although a white Senator guilty of equivalent transgressions, merely was censured. The summer again was marked by uprisings, the worst outbursts occurring in Newark and Detroit, where 66 persons, mostly blacks, were killed.

King turned his attention to the poor in the urban ghettos. He attacked the government's involvement in Vietnam, calling it "one of history's most cruel and senseless wars." Old-line rights leaders criticized him for "muddling" the civil rights issue with the peace issue. King replied in a sermon in New York:

"The war is doing far more than devastating the hopes of the poor at home," he said. "We are sending black young men to guarantee liberties in Southeast Asia which they have not found in East Harlem. On TV we have watched Negro and white soldiers die together for a nation that has been unable to seat them together in the same schools. I speak for the poor of Vietnam whose country is being destroyed. I speak for the poor of America who are paying the double price of smashed hopes and death and corruption in Vietnam. . . . We must stop the war. We are on the side of the wealthy and are making a hell for the poor."

In August, King spoke of organizing a massive nonviolent campaign in the nation's urban ghettos to secure financial help for the poor. "This is something like a last plea to the nation to respond to nonviolence," he explained to reporters. But he failed to get anything moving. In the northern ghettos, he was up against a more subtle form of racism than he had faced in Montgomery, Birmingham and Selma. He was also swimming against the tide. And he was almost alone in his faith in nonviolence. Floyd McKissick voiced the opinion of most militants when he said that it was a "foolish assumption to try to sell nonviolence to the ghettos."

In 1968 King planned a last test for nonviolence, a "Poor People's" March on Washington in the spring. In March, while making preparations for the demonstration, he was invited to Memphis, Tennessee, to help the city's striking garbage collectors win their demands nonviolently. He led a march, which was marred by violence and looting by some of the demonstrators. Deeply disturbed, King scheduled another march and a series of preparatory rallies to stress the importance of nonviolence.

At the first of these rallies, he told his audience about the threats on his life that he had received. "We've got some difficult days ahead," he said. "But it really doesn't matter with me now. Because I've been to the mountain top. . . . And I've looked over, and I've seen the promised land." A heavy spring rain drummed against the metal roof of the church where he was speaking.

"I may not get there with you," he continued, "but I want you to know tonight that we as a people will get to the promised land."

The next evening, April 4, while preparing to leave for dinner and another rally, King was killed on the balcony of his motel by a sniper's bullet. He was 39 years old.

His funeral was a national event, replete with oratory and promises. Ralph Abernathy, King's closest friend and aide, succeeded him as President of SCLC and led the Poor People's March on Washington—to no avail. King's murderer, a small-time hoodlum hungry for notoriety, was caught, pleaded guilty and was sentenced to life imprisonment. In prison, he received hundreds of letters and parcels containing more than $1,500 in small gifts, 182 Wallace-for-President stickers, and 52 Holy Bibles.

In life a symbol, in death a martyr, King and his achievements and failures were soon plastered over with idolatry and sentimentality by the Establishment—both black and white. Some black militants countered—in reaction, perhaps—by equating King with Booker T. Washington. In some ways the two men *were* similar. Both were humorless and pious and had an exaggerated sense of their own roles (King's associates sometimes slyly referred to him as "de Lawd" in private). And both were applauded by the white Establishment. But the similarities end there, as can be seen in the two men's basic philosophies and actions.

Perhaps poet Julius Lester came closest to assessing accurately King's impact upon his times. He said that King unwittingly had made America "show its true face" in its response to nonviolence. It was in this role, he added, "as the unconscious and unwilling instrument of the forces of history," that King's real significance lay.

Even before his death, King had been outstripped by his times, overtaken by events that he no longer could control. Death only had made official his status as a relic of the past to which one pays more homage than attention. Indeed, in death his name commanded more attention than it had in the last years of his life. But, while the Establishment glorified King and nonviolence, the revolution moved along other paths.

"We are not fighting for integration, nor are we fighting for separation. We are fighting for recognition as human beings."

Malcolm X

BLACK NATIONALISM

"Political, social and industrial America will never become so converted as to be willing to share up equitably between black and white," said black nationalist Marcus Garvey in 1923. Garvey, who in the 1920's organized what historian John Hope Franklin has called "the largest Negro movement of its kind in history," had this advice for his fellow blacks:

"If you cannot live alongside the white man in peace, if you cannot get the same chance and opportunity as a white man . . . because the country is his by force of numbers, then find a country of your own. . . ."

Garvey, of course, was not the first to suggest this. For more than 100 years, black nationalists had sought to lead their people out of bondage—spiritual as well as physical—and back to Africa, their ancestral home.

The first important back-to-Africa movement was fostered by a white-controlled organization, the American

Colonization Society, which was organized in 1816. It probably was inspired by the feat of Paul Cuffee, a wealthy black shipowner who in 1815 had carried 38 free blacks to Sierra Leone, a British colony on Africa's west coast. In 1818, the ACS sent 88 free blacks to colonize Liberia, the swampy, malarial lowlands adjacent to Sierra Leone.

The idea of repatriating blacks to Africa appealed to many whites, particularly northerners. Lincoln, as we have seen, thought it a solution to the "Negro problem in America." And for a while, the black man seemed to agree. In the 1850's, 5,000 blacks emigrated to Liberia, driven there by the passage of the Fugitive Slave Law in 1850 and by the lure of Liberia's newly won political independence. But the Civil War, emancipation, and the promise of reconstruction dampened the black man's ardor for distant shores; he came to hope that he might make it in America.

That hope seemed dead by 1877, and such men as Bishop Henry MacNeal Turner, who had fought vainly for equality during reconstruction, sought solace in the idea of repatriation. "I would make Africa a place of refuge," he said, "because I see no other shelter from the stormy blast, from the red tide of persecution, from the horrors of American prejudice."

In 1877 a group of Charleston blacks formed the Liberian Exodus Company to promote not only repatriation but also trade links between black America and Africa. One of the organizers was Martin R. Delany, a physician and writer who before the war had helped to negotiate a treaty with some Nigerian chiefs for the immigration of American blacks. "The white races," Delany had said then, "are but one-third of the population of the globe . . . and it cannot much longer continue that two-thirds will passively submit to the universal domination of the one-third."

The LEC was only one of a number of organizations

that were formed between the late 1870's and World War I to promote black repatriation. Lacking funds and experienced managers, none of them lasted very long. The blacks, themselves, instead of going to Africa, went north to Kansas and Chicago.

But Bishop Turner, as he watched the European colonialists divide Africa among themselves, continued to call for a return to Africa to help stem the colonial tide. Eloquent, single-minded, fiercely proud, he remained the foremost exponent of black repatriation until his death in 1915. A year later, Marcus Garvey, a man not unlike Turner, sailed into New York harbor with a message for American blacks.

Marcus Mosiah Garvey was, as he later put it, "ushered into a world of sin, the flesh and the devil" in 1887 in St. Ann's Bay, a small town on the island of Jamaica. He was the last of eleven children, of whom only one other reached adulthood.

As a boy, Garvey was nicknamed "Mose" or "Ugly Mug." In St. Ann's Bay, he studied and played with both black and white children until he was fourteen years old. At that time, his favorite playmate, a white girl, was sent to school in Scotland. When she left, she told Garvey that her parents had forbidden her to write to him or see him again because he was a "nigger." This was his first taste of prejudice. "It was then," he later wrote, "that I found for the first time that there were different races, each having its own separate and distinct social life."

At school, Garvey recalled, the teachers "studied me and I studied them." But at fourteen he had to leave school to work. His father, a master mason, worked only when he felt like it, often preferring to lock himself in his room and read; as a result, the family, once prosperous, had slid into poverty.

Garvey worked for three years as a printer's apprentice

and learned his trade so well that at the age of seventeen he felt confident enough to leave his hometown for Kingston, the island's capital. Within three years he was a master printer and foreman at one of the largest Jamaican firms. In 1907, the Printer's Union struck for higher wages, and Garvey went out with his men. But the strike was broken; and Garvey, the only foreman who had struck, was blacklisted by the printing companies.

Finally, he got a job with the government printing office. In his spare time, he started a periodical called *Garvey's Watchman*; and when that failed, he helped to organize a political reform club and edited its publication. But he was restless and ambitious, so in 1910 he left Jamaica for more exciting prospects. He drifted from country to country—Costa Rica, Panama, Ecuador, Nicaragua, Honduras, Columbia, Venezuela—working the plantations, the tobacco fields, the mines. Everywhere, he saw black workers exploited. After nearly two years, "sickened with fever and sick at heart," he returned to Jamaica.

A few months later, in 1912, Garvey sailed for Europe "to find out if it was different there." But there, too, he found prejudice. In London, he developed an interest in black Africa and in black America. Ironically, it was Booker T. Washington who inspired Garvey's black nationalism. After reading Washington's autobiography, *Up from Slavery*, Garvey felt the "doom" of being a "race leader" descend upon him. "I asked," he later wrote, " 'where is the black man's Government? Where is his King and his kingdom? Where is his President, his country, and his ambassador, his army, his navy, his men of big affairs?' I could not find them, and then I declared, 'I will help to make them.' "

Describing his excitement at the prospect before him, Garvey added: "My young and ambitious mind led me into flights of great imagination. I saw before me . . . a new world of black men, not peons, serfs, dogs and slaves, but a nation of sturdy men making their impress upon civilization and causing a new light to dawn upon the human race." His brain "afire," he sailed for Jamaica in 1914.

Back in Jamaica, he immediately organized the Universal Negro Improvement Association and African Communities League "to work for the general uplift of the Negro peoples of the world." Garvey designated himself President and Traveling Commissioner of the new organization.

Most Jamaican blacks were at best indifferent to the UNIA, as the Association later was called. Indeed, the influential mulattos of the island, who liked to think of themselves as more white than black, actively opposed the Association. Finding himself a prophet without honor in his own country, Garvey went to America in 1916 "to lecture in the interest of my Association."

He visited 38 states, talked with a number of "so-called black leaders," and discovered that none of them had organized the people. In Harlem, he lectured in churches and talked himself hoarse on street corners, but few people listened to him. He kept talking, however, and by 1917 he had enough followers to organize a New York Division of the UNIA. Just two years later, the American UNIA, with Garvey as its president, claimed more than 2 million members in 30 branches. The numbers probably were inflated, for Garvey was more concerned with effect than with accuracy. But even a tenth of that membership would have made the UNIA the world's largest organization for blacks.

Garvey started another newspaper, *Negro World*, and this one was successful. Poet Claude McKay called it "the best edited colored weekly in New York." A vehicle for Garvey's racial and political pronouncements, it was published weekly from 1918 to 1933, and in its prime it was circulated around the world. It was so potent that many colonial governments in Africa banned it as subversive.

In 1919, Garvey established the Negro Factories Corporation, raising money by selling stock to blacks. The NFC, stated *Negro World*, would "build and operate factories in the big industrial centers of the United States, Central America, the West Indies and Africa to manufacture every marketable commodity." It did develop a number of black-owned businesses: a chain of cooperative grocery stores, some service shops and a publishing house. But its resources were never large enough to let it live up to its promises.

That same year, Garvey began the Black Star Line, which stirred the imaginations of the black people and aroused the hostility of virtually everyone else. To finance the new steamship company, Garvey raised more than $600,000 in cash by the sale of stock, which was available only to blacks. "Through the Black Star Line we will come into trade relations with our brethren on the West Coast of Africa . . ." he told his readers in *Negro World*. The line also would "transport to Liberia and other African countries those Negroes who desire to possess and enjoy the fruits of the richest country on God's green earth."

The company began its operations with three small vessels, the *Yarmouth*, the *Shadyside* and the *Kanawha*. One disaster followed another. The ships, grossly overpriced rusty hulks that unscrupulous agents had foisted on the inexperienced BSL management, kept breaking down. Garvey's own executives proved either incompetent or dishonest, sometimes both. Finally, the *Shadyside* sank at its Hudson River mooring; the disabled *Kanawha* was left to rot in a Cuban port; and the *Yarmouth*, which had cost $165,000, was sold at public auction for $1,625 to satisfy a debt.

Garvey, however, survived. In 1920, the UNIA held in Harlem the First International Convention of the Negro Peoples of the World. It was a dazzling affair, marked by what Garvey's biographer called "all the splendor and pageantry of a medieval coronation." At a time when W.E.B. Du Bois could not attract even 100 delegates to his Pan-African Congress, Garvey drew thousands of delegates from 25 countries. Addressing a rally of 25,000 blacks, including African chiefs in tribal dress, Garvey called for racial pride and African independence, the two themes he was to stress for the rest of his life. Garvey himself was declared "Provisional President" of the imaginary "African Republic."

Later that year, Garvey launched a fund drive for $2,000,000 to build "colleges, universities, industrial plants and railroad tracks" in Liberia. Less than $150,000 of this was raised, and most of it was spent to bail out the rapidly sinking Black Star Line. It was no use. In 1922, the BSL went bankrupt and Garvey was arrested for "fraudulent representations" in the sale of BSL stock through the mails. In 1923 he was brought to trial.

Garvey insisted upon conducting his own defense in court. The case against him was weak, but his flamboyancy and impromptu lectures antagonized the jury. He was convicted, although it was obvious that, as his biographer noted, "the real criminals were the white culprits who had unloaded the rusty hulks on unsuspecting and inexperienced Negroes."

The judge sentenced Garvey to five years in prison, the maximum sentence, another indication that this was, in the words of historian Hollis R. Lynch, "more of a political than a judicial decision." Garvey, no fool, said the same thing. "I was convicted," he told his supporters, "not because anyone was defrauded . . . but because I represented . . . a movement for the real emancipation of my race." He appealed the verdict.

In 1924, while out on bail pending the appeals decision, Garvey continued to direct various projects, but without success. He was a great organizer but a poor administrator. A new steamship company that he tried to float went under. Shortly afterwards, the Liberian government banned the UNIA from the country and confiscated $50,000 worth of construction equipment that the Association had shipped there. In addition, Garvey was attacked increasingly by other black leaders.

Two years earlier, Garvey had infuriated black leaders by his tacit support of the Ku Klux Klan. An advocate of "racial purity" himself, he understood the Klan and admired its lack of hypocrisy. He also thought the Klan's harassment would drive blacks to the UNIA by convincing them of the futility of trying to integrate into white America. But to most black leaders, approval of the Klan was a betrayal. "Garvey," said Du Bois, the Jamaican's severest critic, "is either a lunatic or a traitor."

It would have made no difference. In 1925, Garvey's appeal was rejected, and he was sent to prison. Two years later, he was pardoned by President Coolidge (for whom he had campaigned in 1924) and deported as an undesirable alien. Back in Jamaica, he revitalized the local UNIA and in 1929 held the Sixth International Convention of the Negro Peoples of the World in Kingston. The pageantry and the oratory again were impressive, but behind the scenes Garvey and the leaders of the American UNIA split over the location of the Association's headquarters. It proved to be the beginning of the end of the UNIA. The body had no direction without the head in Jamaica, and the head could not live without the body in America.

Garvey himself fell into obscurity in the 1930's almost

as quickly as he had arisen from it. In 1933, to replace the defunct *Negro World*, he began a monthly magazine, *Black Man*, which he called a "circulating University" for black people. Two years later, he moved his UNIA headquarters to London. There he died in 1940 after a severe stroke.

Events since his death have vindicated him. The two goals he strove for, racial pride and African liberation, have been largely achieved. Black is now beautiful, and only a few African nations remain under colonial domination. If the return of American blacks to Africa that Garvey encouraged never materialized, it was because, as one black explained, they could not return to a place they never had been; they were Americans, not Africans.

Garvey himself never even visited Africa. In any case, he did not intend that all American blacks should return to Africa. "We do not want all the Negroes in Africa," he once said. "Some are no good here, and naturally will be no good there." He wanted American blacks to help build a strong, independent Africa that would give prestige and strength to blacks everywhere.

Vain, bombastic, impulsive, Garvey flashed across the American scene only briefly, but he left behind him the inspiration for today's black nationalism. "You will find ten years from now, or 100 years from now," he told a white audience in 1928, "Garvey was not an idle buffoon but was representing the new vision of the Negro who was looking forward to great accomplishments in the future."

While some black nationalists pressed for a return to Africa, others wanted to establish a black state in America. Like the return-to-Africa movement, the idea of an internal black state was encouraged and supported by many whites. Removal *anywhere* of the troublesome presence within their

Klan Country, 1969. *The New York Times.* "Political, social and industrial America will never become so converted as to be willing to share up equitably between black and white." Marcus Garvey, 1923.

midst would ease their guilt—out of sight, out of mind. As far back as 1795, one white Philadelphian had suggested colonizing free blacks in the Northwest Territory, at that time still largely Indian country. Thomas Jefferson also had considered this idea in 1801, but then had decided the West Indies or Africa would be preferable.

Throughout the 19th century, both blacks and whites continued to agitate for a separate black state, first in Texas, then in Oklahoma. But the proposal never was considered seriously—there was too much profit to be taken out of the land for the white man to set aside a tract of it for ex-slaves. By 1914, only a few black leaders were pressing the idea, with no realistic hope for success. The dream, however, lingered on, and it lives today in the teachings of Elijah Muhammad, leader of the Nation of Islam, better known as the Black Muslims.

Elijah Muhammad was born Elijah Poole in 1897, the seventh of twelve children of a rural Georgia preacher. He barely learned to read and write before he was forced to work in the fields to help support the family. As a young man, he worked in a variety of jobs, mostly as a manual laborer. Unable to tolerate Georgia racism, he moved to Detroit in 1923 and got a job in the Chevrolet factory. In Detroit, he met Wali Farad, the self-annointed Prophet of the self-established Lost–Found Nation of Islam. Farad changed Poole's name to Elijah Muhammad and appointed him assistant minister in the Detroit Temple.

In 1933, Farad disappeared as suddenly and mysteriously as he had appeared in Detroit three years previously, leaving the leadership of the Temple up for grabs. Elijah Muhammad, making his bid, declared that Farad had been Allah, God himself, and that he, Elijah, was his Prophet, the "Messenger of Allah." The idea failed to move the faithful. Indeed, in the beginning, Elijah's following consisted of his mother and his wife and the first six of their eight children.

The following year, Elijah moved to Chicago and organized a second temple. Its membership was so small that meetings were held in the members' homes. Elijah moved again, in 1935, this time to Washington, D.C., where he established another temple. In 1942 he was imprisoned for counseling draft resistance; Muslims, he told his followers, were forbidden to bear arms against anyone whom Allah had not ordered to be killed.

Released in 1946, Elijah returned to Chicago and established his headquarters there. He built up the sect's membership, established several more small temples, and moved into an elegantly furnished, eighteen-room house in one of the better sections of the city. The Muslims do not release membership figures, but the best estimate is that the sect now numbers between 20,000 and 40,000 registered members, with perhaps 50,000 more believers.

Members are subject to strict rules of personal behavior and diet. Liquor and tobacco are forbidden. So is pork, small game, and "soul food"—collard greens, black-eyed peas, cornbread. Muslims must dress neatly, work hard and stay out of trouble. Most of their time is taken up by organized activity—studying, attending meetings, memorizing ritual, spreading the faith. Drugs, idleness, delinquency, any kind of self-destructive behavior or attitude are not tolerated. Elijah's word is absolute law in all matters.

All this is designed to build up discipline, responsibility and self-respect. As Elijah says: "Islam dignifies the black man, and it gives him the desire to be clean, internally and externally, and to have for the first time a sense of dignity."

It also vilifies the "white devil." An incredible Muslim myth asserts that the white man was "grafted" from the black people (who were the original inhabitants of the earth) and set to rule for 6,000 years to test the mettle of the black man. This time is almost up. American blacks are "Asiatic" blacks who have been Muslims since creation; and as members of the Nation of Islam they have been chosen to destroy the present "evil" civilization and redeem the "Black Nation"—which includes all nonwhites.

Such racist mythology is coupled with a demand for land to create a separate black state, "either on this continent or elsewhere." "We have come to the point we must have a home on this earth to call our own," Elijah declared in 1959. But he has indicated, with more realism, that he might settle for less. "As long as we are not allowed to establish a state or territory of our own," he proclaimed in 1962, "we demand not only equal justice under the laws of the United States, but equal employment opportunities—NOW!"

Denouncing the "white devil," and calling for a total

separation of the races, Elijah and his sect reached their zenith in the early 1960's, a few years before nonviolence was discredited and the ghettos exploded. Since then, the Muslims' influence has declined. Both their sudden rise and their subsequent decline can be attributed largely to the life and death of one man: Malcolm X.

Malcolm X, the "angriest Negro in America," was born in 1925 in Omaha, Nebraska. Christened Malcolm Little, he was the seventh of ten children of a Baptist minister. His father, a strapping, fearless man, was a zealous organizer for Marcus Garvey's UNIA. This activity led to his harassment by the Klan in several towns and, finally, in 1931, to his death in East Lansing, Michigan at the hands of "unknown assailants." Malcolm, who inherited his father's strength and courage, later wrote in his brilliant autobiography: "It has always been my belief that I too will die by violence. I have done all that I can to be prepared."

After Mr. Little's death, the family slowly deteriorated. Forced to go on welfare, Malcolm's mother was unable to cope with the humiliation of charity and the constant surveillance of the social workers. In 1937, she broke down and was institutionalized, and her younger children, made wards of the state, were dispersed among friends.

Within a year, Malcolm was ticketed for a reform school. Everyone but he cried. Sent temporarily to a detention home in Mason, he was surprised to be shown to his own room—the first in his life. The couple in charge of the home took a liking to him—"as a mascot I know now," Malcolm later wrote—and instead of forwarding him to reform school sent him to Mason's regular junior high school. "As the 'nigger' of my class," he later recalled, "I was . . . extremely popular—I suppose partly because I was kind of a novelty."

Elected class president, Malcolm was proud. At that time, he said later, "I didn't really have much feeling about being a Negro because I was trying so hard, in every way I could, to be white."

In 1940, Malcolm spent the summer in Boston with his older half-sister, Ella. Boston ghetto life thrilled him, and when he returned to Mason he found himself restless, especially around white people. Then, in school, he experienced what he later called "the first major turning point of my life." He was in the eighth grade.

One of his teachers asked him if he had thought about a career. He hadn't, but he said he'd like to be a lawyer. The teacher looked at Malcolm with surprise and told him that he "had to be realistic about being a nigger. A lawyer," he added, "that's no realistic goal for a nigger. You need to think about something you *can* be. You're good with your hands—making things. . . . Why don't you plan on carpentry?"

Malcolm, who knew he was brighter than most of his white classmates, all of whom had been encouraged even in their most fanciful ambitions, was deeply disturbed. "It was then," he later wrote, "that I began to change—inside." At the end of the school year, he moved to Boston, where Ella had arranged a transfer of custody. It was the end of his formal education.

The streets of Roxbury, the Boston ghetto, were his high school; later, Harlem was his college. In Roxbury, his friends taught him that "everything in this world is a hustle." He started drinking, smoking marijuana, gambling —and hustling liquor, pot and girls to whites out on the town and the black musicians who entertained them. He bought a zoot suit and straightened, or "conked," his reddish curly hair. It was a painful process. "This," he recalled, "was my first really big step toward self-degradation: when

I endured all of that pain, literally burning my flesh to have it look like a white man's hair."

From Roxbury he graduated to Harlem. Immediately, he was at home. "This world was where I belonged," he later said. For him, there was only one course: "I was going to become one of the most depraved, parasitical hustlers among New York's eight million people—four million of whom work, and the other four million of whom live off them." He did. Dope, numbers, bootleg liquor, prostitution, perversion, burglary—he was in them all, for kicks and profit. "I was a true hustler," he said in the autobiography —"uneducated, unskilled at anything honorable, and I considered myself nervy and cunning enough to live by my wits, exploiting any prey that presented itself. I would risk just about anything."

As he became more deeply involved with Harlem's underworld, he began carrying a gun. Before he had to use it, however, he left Harlem and returned to Roxbury, where he organized a burglary ring. The ring was successful, but Malcolm got careless and all but one of the members were arrested. Early in 1946, Malcolm was sentenced to ten years in prison. He was not yet 21 years old.

Two years later, he was converted to Elijah Muhammad's Black Muslims. Prison was one of the principal breeding grounds of Muslim converts. The reason, Malcolm explained, was that "among all Negroes, the black convict is the most perfectly preconditioned to hear the words, 'the white man is the devil.'"

After he arrived in prison, Malcolm had begun reading and studying; converted, he dedicated himself to books and ideas as he once had dedicated himself to hustling. He read everything he could lay his hands on. To improve his reading and writing skills, he copied out the entire dictionary, a page a day. His thoughts soared; for the first time in his life he felt free. "I knew right there in prison," he said, "that reading had changed forever the course of my life."

The change was complete. He stopped smoking, gave up pork, and vowed to devote the rest of his life to "telling the white man about himself—or die."

In 1952, Malcolm was paroled. He bought a pair of eyeglasses, a suitcase and a watch and went to live in Detroit, where his brother had found him a job as a furniture salesman. While taking personal instruction in the Nation of Islam at the Detroit Temple, Malcolm received his "X" and discarded the surname his "slave masters" had given him. He proved so devoted to his new faith, and so adept at recruiting for it, that in 1953 Elijah named him assistant minister of the Detroit Temple.

Shortly afterward, Malcolm quit his job to devote his full time to the Muslims. Elijah gave him personal instruction in Muslim ritual and doctrine and in temple administration, then sent him to Boston as a full minister to recruit for the faith. In March 1954, Minister Malcolm organized Temple Eleven in Boston; three months later, he organized Temple Twelve in Philadelphia. Elijah rewarded him with the leadership of Temple Seven in New York.

The New York Temple became Malcolm's base, but most of his time was spent crisscrossing the country helping to establish new temples—or Mosques, as they later were called—in different cities. He was very good at his job. When he began organizing in 1954, he noted, "one bus couldn't have been filled with the Muslims in New York City" and "not more than 500 white people in all of America knew we existed." In less than ten years, Malcolm had established two new Mosques in New York and had organized close to 100 more in 50 states, and the Muslims had become the bogeymen of white America.

Malcolm preached Elijah's message of separation, but with a charisma and brilliance that the Messenger himself never could achieve. He demanded land and independence for the black man and denounced the white man, Christianity, integration, intermarriage, and even civil rights legislation.

"I can't turn around without hearing about some 'civil rights advance,'" he would say. "White people seem to think the black man ought to be shouting 'hallelujah!' Four hundred years the white man has had his foot-long knife in the black man's back—and now the white man starts to *wiggle* the knife out, maybe six inches! The black man's supposed to be grateful? Why if the white man jerked the knife *out,* it's still going to leave a *scar!*"

Even Martin Luther King was moved by Malcolm's cold intensity. "I just saw Malcolm X on television," he once told a friend. "I can't deny it. When he starts talking about all that's been done to us, I get a twinge of hate, of identification with him."

Malcolm's increasing notoriety, however, especially among young people, kindled Elijah's jealousy. In 1962, Malcolm noticed that less and less appeared about him in the Muslim's paper, *Muhammad Speaks*, which he himself had founded. Other signs indicated Elijah's pique, but Malcolm tried to ignore them. "I *loved* the Nation and Mr. Muhammad. I *lived for* the Nation, and for Mr. Muhammad," he wrote.

Even when it became clear that Elijah had violated the strict sexual morality that he had prescribed for Muslims, Malcolm remained dedicated. But his fate already had been decided in Chicago. In November 1963, Elijah suspended Malcolm from the Muslims for 90 days, allegedly for a remark he had made about President Kennedy's assassination. Several days later, Malcolm heard of talk in his own Mosque of killing him. "And then I knew," he wrote in his autobiography, "as any official in the Nation of Islam would have instantly known, any death talk for me could have been approved of—if not actually initiated—by only one man."

Shortly afterward, Malcolm learned that the order for his assassination actually had been issued. The Muslim assigned to carry out the order had gone instead to Malcolm. This direct death order triggered Malcolm's "psychological divorce" from the Black Muslims. He formed his own organization, Muslim Mosque, Inc. It would be "the working base for an action program designed to eliminate the political oppression, the economic exploitation, and the social degradation suffered daily by 22 million Afro-Americans." Now calling himself El-Hajj Malik El-Shabazz, he made a pilgrimage to Mecca to expose himself to the "true Islam."

He was surprised by the absence of any "color problem" in Mecca. And when his host, a prominent Moslem who "would have been considered white in America," went out of his way to accommodate him, Malcolm "began to reappraise the 'white man.'" Returning to America after a triumphant tour of Africa, he told the press: "The true Islam has shown me that a blanket indictment of all white people is as wrong as when whites make blanket indictments against blacks."

A few weeks after his return, Malcolm formed the Organization of Afro-American Unity, a black nationalist organization dedicated to the fight for human rights and dignity. He now saw things "on a broader scale." In speeches around the country, mostly before college audiences, he tried to clarify his new position. Defending himself against the charge that he encouraged violence he said:

"That is a lie. I'm not for wanton violence, I'm for justice." But, he insisted, "our people are within their rights to protect themselves by whatever means necessary. A man with a rifle or a club can only be stopped by a person who defends himself with a rifle or club."

On another occasion, he explained: "I don't speak against the sincere, well-meaning good white people. I have learned that there *are* some. I have learned that not all white people are racists. I am speaking against and my fight is against the white *racists*."

His thinking broadened further as his contacts expanded. After a conversation with one American ambassador, he decided that "the white man is *not* inherently evil, but America's racist society influences him to act evilly." This society, he said, fostered a way of thinking that brought out the worst in people.

When he was asked what white people of good will could do, Malcolm replied that they "had to combat, actively and directly, the racism in other white people." Their place was "not among the black *victims*, but out on the battle lines where America's racism really *is*—and that's in their own home communities . . . among their fellow whites."

Just after his break with Elijah, Malcolm had stated that "we are not fighting for integration, nor are we fighting for separation. We are fighting for recognition as human beings." Almost a year later, he concluded that "we have to approach the black man's struggle against the white man's racism as a human problem." He had come a long way and seemed ready to go much further.

But, for Malcolm, the past was closing in rapidly. In early February 1965, a flaming Molotov cocktail was hurled through the front window of his home, burning half the house down. A week later, Malcolm himself was cut down by a hail of bullets while addressing a meeting in New York. He was dead on arrival at the hospital. Three black men, two of them Muslims, later were arrested, convicted of Malcolm's murder and sentenced to life imprisonment.

"For the Negroes in America," said historian C. Eric Lincoln, "the death of Malcolm X is the most portentous event since the deportation of Marcus Garvey in the 1920's." In fact, Malcolm's death was a loss for all Americans, white as well as black. Malcolm had lived at least two lives and had embarked on a third when he was killed. He had spent one life as a hustler, another as Elijah's disciple. Actually, the two were not unrelated. It could be said that, as Elijah's disciple, Malcolm, without realizing it, simply had changed his hustle. For twelve years, he "adored" Elijah. Near the end, however, when Malcolm reflected on his relationship with the self-styled Messenger of Allah, he noted: "I was going downhill until he picked me up, but the more I think of it, we picked each other up."

His third life had promised to bear less bitter fruit. Having renounced his hatred as well as his vices, he had begun to work for the creation of a society "in which there could exist honest white–black brotherhood." With his death, the road to that society seemed that much longer.

"We're forced to become revolutionaries, since they program us right out of the system."

*A forty-eight-year-old lawyer
in Pontiac, Michigan*

REBELLION IN THE GHETTOS

The loss of Malcolm was felt deeply by blacks, particularly in the ghettos. Malcolm had been one of them, and he had expressed the deep anger they felt, the anger that King had tried to turn into love.

Most whites did not realize the depth of that anger. To them the black ghetto was a set of depressing statistics: high rates of unemployment, disease, death, prostitution, crime, and drug addiction. But life there was so outside the whites' experience, even beyond their comprehension, they didn't concern themselves with it. They blotted it from their consciousness until, like a dormant volcano, the ghetto erupted and reminded them of its presence.

Between 1900 and 1910, six major race riots broke out in American cities, including the one in Springfield, Illinois that led to the formation of the NAACP. In 1917, a bloody riot in East St. Louis left 48 dead and more than 300 injured. That same year, black soldiers in Houston, goaded by white civilians, killed seventeen of their tormentors.

In the last six months of 1919, riots erupted in 25 cities, an average of almost a riot a week. The most violent was in Chicago, where a week of street fighting left 38 dead and 537 injured and destroyed the homes of about 1,000 black families. In most instances the fighting was touched off by some incident, real or imagined. But the incident itself was not important because beneath the surface the ghetto seethed constantly and the incident merely released long pent-up pressure. "At the bottom of the social heap," said Malcolm X, "is the black man in the ghetto. He lives night and day with the rats and the cockroaches. . . . He has nothing to lose, even his life, because he didn't have that in the first place."

The black ghetto erupted again in 1943 in Detroit and New York. Forty people died, hundreds more were injured, and millions of dollars of property was destroyed. Then, during the next 20 years, the black man sought to improve his status through nonviolent demonstrations.

Real progress was made, but not enough. Despite the Supreme Court's 1954 edict, most schools—especially those in the ghettos— still were segregated ten years later. The civil rights legislation that was passed was inadequately enforced. Funds that were promised to the "War on Poverty" were shifted instead to the war in Vietnam. Housing remained segregated; employment remained discriminatory, especially in such trades as construction, where lack of education, the usual reason given for not employing blacks, does not apply.

Few of the benefits of the nonviolent revolution trickled down to the ghetto blacks. The young people particularly were undereducated, unemployed and harassed by the police. In Eldridge Cleaver's words, they were "turned off to the system." They felt walled in—as indeed they were.

Protester on the Capitol steps. Photograph by Jill Freedman.
Old News: Resurrection City. The Poor came to Washington,
but the War on Poverty had become the War in Vietnam.

In 1964, some of the frustration surfaced and violence flared in eight American cities. Little changed, however. Then, in the summer of 1965, Watts, Los Angeles' black ghetto, exploded in rebellion.

In five days of violence, 35 people were killed, 1,080 were injured, 4,310 were arrested. A mob of 10,000 blacks set fire to automobiles and buildings, looted stores and exchanged shots with policemen. Property damage was estimated at $35 million, far more than the damage from all racial disturbances of the previous five years. As columns of smoke spiraled above Los Angeles, angry blacks cried, "Burn, baby, burn!"

White America was shocked. Why Watts? people asked. Ten months earlier *Reader's Digest* had published an article, "How Los Angeles Eases Racial Tensions." And, in a 1964 "statistical portrait," the Urban League had ranked Los Angeles first among 68 cities in terms of housing and employment for blacks. Neither of these pulse-takers, however, could be said to be in touch with the ghetto. There, housing, although perhaps statistically noteworthy, still was substandard. There, the unemployment rate for blacks, although lower than in most cities, still was double or triple that for whites. And there, a racist police chief lumped "crime and civil rights demonstrations" into the same category.

An official commission of six whites and two blacks, reporting on "the meaning of the incredible events" in Watts, recommended "expanded community relations programs" and "continuing urban rehabilitation and renewal." The War on Poverty belatedly turned its guns on Watts.

The biggest gun in the War on Poverty was the Economic Opportunity Act (EOA), which had become law in 1964. Its funds were dispersed by the Office of Economic Opportunity (OEO), which administered programs for adults, for young people and for communities. The OEO also funded Volunteers in Service to America (VISTA), a kind of domestic Peace Corps, which was involved in all three types of programs.

The OEO hastily funneled $70 million dollars into the Economic and Youth Opportunities Agency of Greater Los Angeles (EYOA). But, what with bureaucratic red tape, petty politics, mismanagement and overpaid administrators and "consultants," little of this money found its way to the poor. And each succeeding year the funds were cut back. The result, five years later: housing and education in Watts still were substandard, the police still were hostile, unemployment still was triple that for whites. "They gave us just enough to whet our appetites, then there was no more," said one local black leader in 1970. Then he added, ominously: "Next time, Beverly Hills is gonna burn, not Watts. Because these people here are frustrated."

In the summer of 1966, violence broke out in more than a dozen cities, in many instances triggered by clashes between black citizens and the police. Seven people, all blacks, were killed in Chicago and Cleveland before National Guard troops were able to restore order. The white "backlash" stiffened, and as it did, pressure built up in the black ghettos.

That pressure exploded in the summer of 1967 in another dozen or so cities, most tragically in rebellions in Newark, New Jersey and Detroit, Michigan.

Newark, a depressed, deteriorating city with a history of municipal corruption and brutal police action against blacks, erupted first. Not surprisingly, the rebellion was triggered—and later fanned—by police insensitivity. In five days of shooting, looting and burning, 23 people died, 21 of them blacks. Trigger-happy police, state troopers and National Guardsmen killed all but two or three of the blacks—some of them in cold blood.

Ten million dollars worth of property, most of it retail

goods, was destroyed or stolen. But the looters were very selective in their targets. Stores owned by blacks and identified by signs reading "Soul Brother" were not disturbed. It remained for policemen and troopers to walk down the streets and deliberately smash the windows of perhaps 100 of these stores as the action slowed.

Less than a week after the Newark rebellion was quelled, the black ghetto in Detroit exploded. Detroit, one-third of its population black, was considered a model city in its handling of race relations. Only two weeks before the uprising, Detroit businessmen had told the head of a group active in urban affairs that the city was progressing well in aiding ghetto residents. From the perspective of the ghetto, however, the view was different. "The *Man* got his foot on my back and I can't breathe," complained one unemployed black worker.

As in Newark, the violence in Detroit was provoked by police action. The death and destruction that followed, however, made Newark, and even Watts, look like rehearsals for the real thing. In five bloody days, 43 persons died, 33 of them blacks. More than 2,000 others were injured and about 7,000 more were arrested. At the height of the rebellion, as smoke poured out of burning tenements, United States Army tanks rumbled along the ghetto streets spraying anything that moved with .50 calibre machine gun bullets.

Property damage was estimated at $85 million. When the smoke cleared, Detroit's Mayor Jerome P. Cavanaugh said of the ghetto: "It looks like Berlin in 1945."

In Detroit, too, most of the dead were victims of the police and troops. Several policemen later were accused of "executing" three black teenagers in what became known as the "Algiers Motel incident," but in court they were acquitted by an all-white jury. "This latest phase of a step-by-step whitewash of police slaying," a black state senator said of the verdict, "demonstrates once again that law and order is a one way street. There is no law and order when black people are involved, especially when they're involved with the police."

After the holocaust, Detroit's business and government leaders promised to correct the abuses that underlay the rebellion—heavy unemployment, substandard housing, police bigotry. But, three years later, *The New York Times* reported: "The pledges of July 1967 are unredeemed. . . . And today the polarization between blacks and whites appears sharper, while white liberals have largely abandoned the central city, giving up influence and interest."

That assessment confirmed the observation of the National Advisory Commission on Civil Disorders appointed by President Johnson to study the causes and implications of the rebellions. In the spring of 1968, the Commission had concluded: "Our nation is moving toward two societies, one black, one white—separate and unequal."

The rebellions in Watts, Newark and Detroit revealed how far the nonviolent revolution had fallen short of its goals. It had integrated trains and buses, theaters, restaurants and hotels, particularly in the South. But nonviolent tactics had failed to integrate schools, housing or jobs in either the South or the North. And the prospect of reform in these vital areas was receding daily. White Americans were slipping back into their comfortable pockets of complacency; some were saying that the black man had gone too far too fast. Most white people, said Martin Luther King, Jr., were "uneasy with injustice but unwilling yet to pay a significant price to eradicate it."

This message came across to black people. It produced not only the rebellions but also disillusionment with nonviolence among blacks in CORE and SNCC, the two leading activist rights organizations. In March 1966, Floyd B. McKissick succeeded James Farmer as National Director of CORE. McKissick, a tall, aggressive forty-four-year-old lawyer from North Carolina, quickly made CORE more militant. "Forget about civil rights," he said. "I'm talking about black power."

McKissick brought CORE into the ghettos and phased out the role of white leadership in the organization. Many of CORE's white supporters were offended, and financial contributions to the organization shrank. But McKissick stood fast. In 1967 the word "multiracial" was dropped from the description of CORE. The civil rights movement was "dead," McKissick declared, and in its place a "black revolution" had emerged. The time had come, he added, "when black people have got to support their own organizations."

This didn't mean that whites were barred from the organization, McKissick insisted; but other CORE officials said that the change in description would "let the world know the direction that CORE is going."

That direction became even more evident in 1968, when thirty-four-year-old Roy Innis, an outspoken advocate of black power and black nationalism, succeeded McKissick as National Director. Within two years, CORE officially had forsaken integration for black separatism, and Innis was predicting an "all-out war" with the old line civil rights leaders and the "activist-bureaucrats" of the Department of Health, Education and Welfare (HEW).

Ironically, one of those "activist-bureaucrats" was James Farmer, the former leader of CORE who in 1969 had accepted appointment by President Nixon to the post of Assistant Secretary of HEW.

SNCC's leadership also changed hands in the spring of

1966. The organization itself had changed considerably since the days when it merely coordinated the nonviolent activities of student groups. By 1965 SNCC consisted of a staff of more than 200 professional organizers, many of them former student demonstrators who had remained in the front lines of the battle. They had elected twenty-five-year-old John Lewis, one of the founders of SNCC, chairman of the organization in the spring of 1965. The following spring, Lewis was reelected, then suddenly challenged by a group of SNCC militants led by Stokely Carmichael, a twenty-five-year-old graduate of Howard University and admirer of Malcolm X.

At issue was whether or not to exclude whites from SNCC. Carmichael, gifted, articulate, persuasive, with a deep distrust of whites, argued for their exclusion. Black people, he explained, especially rural blacks, are intimidated by the presence of whites because of the power the white man holds over their lives. Therefore an honest dialogue between blacks and whites is impossible. Black people, he felt, had to "cut themselves off from whites," have their own organizations, write their own histories.

He acknowledged that whites had played an important role in the black movement, but that role, he said, was now over. It was time for a showdown with racism. "The civil rights movement was good because it demanded that blacks be admitted into the system," he said. "Now we must move beyond the stage of demanding entry, to the new stage of changing the system itself."

Carmichael's arguments prevailed, forcing the ouster of Lewis only a few hours after he had been reelected. Six weeks later, Lewis resigned from SNCC, explaining: "I'm not prepared to give up my personal commitment to nonviolence."

Carmichael no longer had such a commitment. A veteran of the sit-ins and freedom rides, he had been harassed and insulted, slugged and jailed. The white man's abuses, and white America's hypocrisy, had ground down his idealism. "I'm not in the movement out of love," he said. "I'm in the movement because I hate. I hate racism, and I'm out to smash it or it's going to smash me."

Within six weeks, Carmichael was a national figure. James Meredith, the first black graduate of the University of Mississippi, was shot and wounded attempting a lone "freedom march" from Memphis, Tennessee, to Jackson, Mississippi. King, McKissick and Carmichael then rallied about 1,500 marchers to finish Meredith's proposed journey. They marched into Greenwood, Mississippi, where Carmichael made an impassioned speech calling for "black power" to combat Mississippi racism. The phrase caught on immediately and made Carmichael the new bogeyman of white America.

Black power, King once said, means different things to different people and even different things to the same person on differing occasions. Few of these meanings, however, have thrown much light on the subject. White Americans, feeling vaguely uneasy, read into it the threat of violence. And old-line civil rights leaders, tied financially and politically to the white Establishment, dismiss black power as divisive, demagogic or worse. For a more enlightening view, one must look to black militants like McKissick, who said black power simply means "putting power in black people's hands. We don't have any and we want some."

Carmichael, the theorist of the movement, was even more explicit than McKissick. He explained how black power related historically and philosophically to the black man's experience in white America.

Black people, he wrote in a brilliant essay, *Toward*

Police barricade. Photograph by Jill Freedman. *Old News: Resurrection City.* "A man with a rifle or a club can only be stopped by a person who defends himself with a rifle or club." Malcolm X.

Black Liberation, are defined by two qualities: their blackness and their powerlessness. Excluded from participation in power, they have been kept dependent and subservient to the white community by every institution of American society. Carmichael called this institutionalized racism, as opposed to individual prejudice.

For example, he explained, the bombing in 1963 of a

church in Birmingham killing five black children was an act of individual racism that most people, white as well as black, deplored. But in the same city, 500 ghetto babies die each year from lack of proper food, shelter and medical care, and white society, although it has the power to change these conditions, does not. That is institutionalized racism.

All black ghettos are the same, Carmichael noted—"the result of identical patterns of white racism, which repeat themselves in cities as distant as Boston and Birmingham." To correct this pattern of economic exploitation, political impotence and discrimination in employment and education, requires "far-reaching changes in the basic power relationships and the ingrained social patterns within the society." How can it be done?

In the past, most articulate blacks and their white allies sought social justice by "integrating the Negro into the mainstream." It was significant, Carmichael pointed out, that this solution was always formulated "in terms of 'the Negro,' the individual Negro, rather than in terms of the community.

"This concept of integration," he added, "had to be based on the assumption that there was nothing of value in the Negro community... so the thing to do was to siphon off the 'acceptable' Negroes into the surrounding middle-class white community. Thus the goal of the movement for integration was simply to loosen up the restrictions barring the entry of Negroes into the white community."

The black community remained dependent, Carmichael noted, relying for its salvation on an appeal "to the conscience of white institutions of power." It created political leverage by forming coalitions with various "liberal" white pressure organizations—labor unions, church and civic groups, political parties.

But this had failed. "Political alliances based on appeals to conscience and decency," he said, "are chancy things, simply because institutions and political organizations have no consciences outside their own special interests. The political and social rights of Negroes have been and always will be negotiable and expendable the moment they conflict with the interests of our 'allies.' "

The goal of integration, Carmichael concluded, was neither realistic nor particularly desirable. Even if it could be achieved, the result would be to drain the black community of its most talented citizens until eventually it was abolished.

"The fact is," he added, "that what must be abolished is not the black community but the dependent colonial status that has been inflicted upon it. The racial and cultural personality of the black community must be preserved, and the community must win its freedom while preserving its cultural integrity. This is the essential difference between integration as it is currently practiced and the concept of black power."

Carmichael left to others the practical implementation of black power. After serving as SNCC chairman for a year, he traveled to London, then to Cuba and North Vietnam, where he was welcomed as a spokesman for black revolutionaries. Indeed, in London he broadened the concept of black power and related it to "liberation struggles around the world." And, in Havana, he declared: "We have no other alternative but to take up arms and struggle for our total liberation and total revolution in the United States."

In 1968, Carmichael was named Prime Minister of the Black Panther Party, a militant nationalist group that had sprung up on the West Coast. A year later, however, unable to agree with the Panthers' policy of cooperating with whites, he resigned his post and went to live in Guinea. "I know that I cannot provide the leadership right now in America," he said. "I do not know how to begin to cope with the problems. . . ." Then, in February 1971, he declared: "The black man should no longer be thinking of transforming American society. We should be concerned with Mother Africa."

His successor as chairman of SNCC was Hubert G. Brown, better known as H. Rap Brown, a gangling twenty-four-year-old firebrand from Baton Rouge, Louisiana. He took over the post in the spring of 1967.

The new chairman lacked Carmichael's polish, but he quickly proved he could match his predecessor's revolutionary rhetoric. "Violence is necessary," he told reporters in July 1967, as the ashes in Newark and Detroit still were cooling. "It is as American as cherry pie." Then he shouted to about 100 assembled blacks: "I say you better get you a gun. The honky [white man] got respect for but one thing, a gun."

Less than a year later, Brown himself was fined $2,000 and sentenced to five years in jail for carrying a rifle on an airline flight between New York and New Orleans. He appealed the sentence. That same year SNCC decided to decentralize, and Brown stepped down as chairman. But, in July 1969, he resumed the post and SNCC dropped the word "nonviolent" from its name, replacing it with "national." "If the situation demands that you retaliate violently," Brown explained, "you would no longer be hindered or hampered by 'nonviolent' in the organization's name."

A few months later, Brown was ordered to stand trial on charges of arson and inciting to riot in Cambridge, Maryland.* In a fiery speech in Cambridge a few days after the Detroit holocaust, he had said that "if this town don't

---

* A Maryland prosecutor later admitted to reporters that a fellow prosecutor had told him that he had "fabricated" an arson charge against Brown so the FBI could be called in if Brown ever should flee. (Arson is a felony, and an FBI fugitive warrant can be obtained only for fugitives from felony charges.)

come around [to black militant demands] this town should be burnt down." A few hours later, parts of Cambridge did burn, but only after the police, without provocation, had fired a shotgun blast at a peaceful group of blacks, wounding several, including Brown.

At the time of his arrest on the charge, Brown declared: "I consider myself neither morally nor legally bound to obey laws made by a body in which I have no representation."

Brown left New York in the spring of 1970, reportedly to drive to Maryland for the trial, but he never arrived. At the time, two SNCC workers were blown to pieces in their car in Maryland, and Brown's friends believed his life also was in danger. He probably went underground. But if anybody knew, he was not talking. "We don't know whether Rap Brown is alive or dead," his attorney, William Kunstler told reporters. A few weeks later, the FBI added Brown's name to its list of the "Ten Most Wanted" fugitives.

The foremost advocate of black power was in exile, his successor was a fugitive, and SNCC itself had all but ceased to function. But pride in blackness and the idea of black control of black communities, seeds which Garvey had sown and Malcolm X had watered, were in full flower. Blacks were speaking for themselves, defining themselves, organizing themselves. And, in another outgrowth of Malcolm's black nationalism, they were learning about themselves in "black studies" programs in top universities across the country.

Like black power, black studies also generated friction between the races. The first such program was introduced at San Francisco State College in 1966. At least three questions—the content and purpose of the program, black control of it, and white participation in it—became issues shortly afterward.

In 1968, at San Francisco State, Black Studies Coordinator Dr. Nathan Hare, a sociologist, insisted that "black today is revolutionary and nationalistic. A Black Studies program which is not revolutionary and nationalistic is, therefore . . . irrelevant."

That same year about 50 black militants at Cornell stormed into a meeting of the planning committee of the university's Afro-American Studies Program and took over. "Our aim," they proclaimed, "is the creation of a Black College of black students and scholars within a white university, which will deal with the problems of Black America." White students later burned a cross in front of a black women's dormitory, and a group of black militants retaliated by seizing the student union building and arming themselves with rifles. Only a hurriedly negotiated truce between blacks and university officials prevented bloodshed.

In 1969, a student at Antioch College in Ohio explained why the school's Afro-American Studies Institute barred white teachers and students. "For a white student to be in any of these sessions," he said, "would only blunt the knife, and inhibit fundamental emotions from being expressed."

Not all blacks, however, agreed. Roy Wilkins of the NAACP called such policies "another version of segregation and Jim Crow." And Dr. Kenneth Clark, a trustee of Antioch, resigned from the board when Antioch approved the Institute's exclusion of whites. "It is whites who need a black studies program most of all," he said. Such a "black separatist" policy, he added, reinforced "the Negro's inability to compete with whites for the real power of the real world."

In the schools, themselves, opinion split along racial lines.

Some whites approved, but more were indifferent or vaguely disapproved of the blacks' militance. Black students, however, were enthusiastic.

"There's a feeling I can say whatever I like, or don't like, about white society—or about black society, for that matter," said one Cornell student. "The bonus is that I feel the instructor understands, without my having to translate it." A student leader at Harvard explained: "We want to understand the system so we can go about changing it, and we want to learn the skills that will help us change it." And the head of the Black Student Union at Berkeley pointed out what may be the most significant role of these programs. Black studies, he said, "is a bridge between people who have expertise and those who need it most desperately, the people in the ghetto."

The ghetto, where the direction of the black revolution is likely to be determined, is where the action is today. Ghetto blacks still seethe with anger. But they also now breathe defiance and determination to do something about their condition, as is indicated by the history of the Black Panther Party, which was founded in 1966 by two black nationalists, Bobby Seale and Huey P. Newton.

Seale, a native of Dallas, grew up in the Southwest and Berkeley, California. His parents were poor and the Air Force offered an escape from poverty, so he enlisted. After almost four years in the service, he received a bad conduct discharge for insubordination. He was not, however, an activist at that time. "Before I went to college," he said later, "when I was in the service, I wasn't aware of civil rights. . . ."

After his discharge, he worked at aircraft plants as a mechanic and took some courses at Merritt Junior College in Oakland, where he became fascinated by black history.

At Merritt, he also met Huey Newton, who helped him to develop a black nationalist perspective on the "things I'd seen in the black community."

Newton, a minister's son, grew up in the Oakland ghetto. His early interests were history, psychology, sociology, and law. "I was lucky," he said recently, "I knew the block, and I knew the book."

Seale and Newton met in 1962. Four years later, in an antipoverty center in Oakland, they wrote out a ten-point platform and program for what they first named the Black Panther Party for Self-Defense. When they were finished, Newton said to Seale: "We've got to have some kind of structure. What do you want to be, chairman or minister of defense?"

"Doesn't make any difference to me," Seale replied.

"I'll be the minister of defense," Newton decided, "and you'll be the chairman."

At the time, Seale was 30 years old, Newton, 25.

Few newspapers ever printed the Panther's ten-point program, preferring instead to dwell on the party's more sensational activities. But it is difficult to evaluate the Panthers' rhetoric and actions without some knowledge of the thinking behind them.

The first three points of the program call for "power to determine the destiny of our Black Community," for full employment and for restitution "for slave labor and mass murder of black people." Points four, five and six demand decent housing, "education that teaches us our true history and our role in the present day society" and exemption for blacks from military service for "a racist government that does not protect us." The next three points demand "an immediate end to POLICE BRUTALITY and MURDER of black people," freedom for all black prisoners (because they did not receive a fair trial) and trial of blacks by black juries. Police brutality would be fought by "organizing black self-defense groups." The tenth point calls for a United Nations-supervised vote of black Americans to determine their destiny.

Since 1966, the Panthers have become more of a "socialist organization," that believes "that the means of protection should be in the hands of the people." Newton in an interview in 1968 declared: "We have two evils to fight, capitalism and racism."

The Panthers not only theorized, they acted. Dressed in black leather jackets and black berets and toting rifles and shotguns, Panthers "patrolled" the ghetto streets to discourage police brutality, which in the Oakland ghetto, as in every black ghetto, was a long-standing problem. The Panthers also opened free health clinics and special classes for ghetto youths and began a free breakfast program for hungry children. They soon won support in black communities across the country.

One of their early converts was Eldridge Cleaver, an ex-convict, best selling author and disciple of Malcolm X. Cleaver, a native of Little Rock, had spent almost half his life in California reform schools and prisons. He had become a Black Muslim in prison, but had renounced the Muslims when Malcolm was expelled and murdered. Paroled in 1967, Cleaver, then 32 years old, became the Panthers' minister of information when he discovered how close Newton and Seale were to Malcolm's thinking.

With Malcolm X dead and Stokely Carmichael retired, the Panthers quickly became the prime target of police departments across the country. "Provocation, false arrests, trumped-up charges, illegal detention, barbaric treatment, excessive bail and even legal murder—this [was] everyday treatment for the Panthers," said political scientist Ronald Steel.

The record appears to bear him out.

In October 1967, Oakland police provoked an incident with Newton in which one policeman was killed and Newton and another policeman were wounded. Newton was convicted of manslaughter and sent to prison for two to fifteen years, but in 1970 the conviction was overturned and Newton was released on bail pending a new trial.

In January 1968, Oakland police forced their way into Cleaver's apartment at 3:00 A.M. without a search warrant and held Cleaver and his wife at gunpoint while they looked for something incriminating. They found nothing. A few weeks later, at 3:30 A.M., they did the same thing to Bobby Seale. Again, they were disappointed.

But that was only the beginning. In the next two years, at least seven Panthers were shot dead by police in Oakland, Chicago, Los Angeles and Seattle. The most notorious incidents occurred in Oakland and Chicago. In a shoot-out in Oakland in 1968, police forced the surrender of Cleaver (who had no gun) and Bobby Hutton, the seventeen-year-old treasurer of the Panthers. As the two Panthers gave themselves up, hands held high, Hutton was gunned down in cold blood. The killing was ruled "justifiable homicide."

A year later, fourteen Chicago policemen killed two Panthers and wounded four others after bursting into their apartment at 4:00 A.M. The police claimed that the Panthers fired at them. But no police were wounded and all the bullet holes were found where the victims were slain; and of 83 shells accounted for, 82 of them were from police guns. One of the victims, Fred Hampton, had been shot in bed. These killings also were ruled "justifiable."

There have been many other similar incidents. They are approved or at least accepted, by most Americans because, as Steel said, the Panthers "have been defined as threatening to white society and, therefore, beyond the normal protection of the law." The FBI, for example, has branded the Panthers as the "most dangerous and violence-prone of all extremist groups." Yet, when the question of violence is raised with Newton, he replies: "We've never advocated violence. Violence is inflicted upon us. But we do believe in self-defense for ourselves and for black people." A fine distinction perhaps, but worth pondering.

Newton also lays to rest the myth that the Panthers, because they are an all-black organization, are antiwhite. In fact, they are virtually the only black militant organization that actually welcomes white allies—so long as they don't try to dictate policy to them. "We don't hate white people," Newton says, "we hate the oppressor."

The future of the party itself, however, remains uncertain. In 1968 Cleaver's parole was revoked, despite the fact that he had not violated it. He fled to Algiers rather than return to prison, where he was sure an "accidental" death awaited him at the hands of his former guards. In Algiers, Cleaver established an international Panther headquarters, then in 1971, he quarrelled publicly with Newton. "The party is in turmoil just as this country is in turmoil," Newton admitted. "There are contradictions in the party just as there are contradictions in the world."

The dispute appeared to be over the means of liberating political prisoners like Angela Davis (on trial in California for her life for allegedly supplying the murder weapon in a kidnap-murder) and George Jackson (the "Soledad Brother" now in the eleventh year of a one-year-to-life sentence for a $70.00 robbery). Cleaver favors revolutionary action such as exchanging hostages for the prisoners. Newton wants to continue organizing the black community around the party's ten-point program and take his chances. "We can't free all political prisoners until the people are free," he says. "Free the community and they

From *Black in White America*. Photograph by Leonard Freed.
© Magnum Photos, Inc.

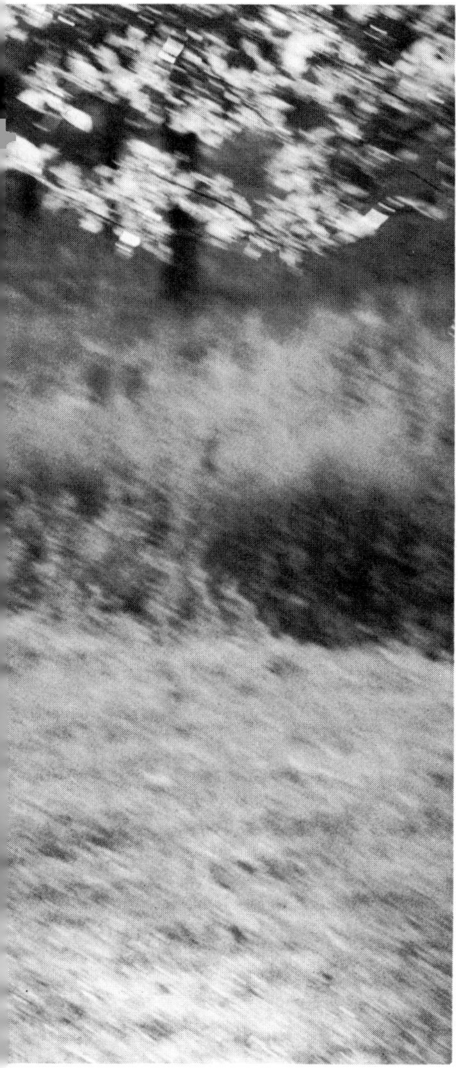

will free all political prisoners."

Meanwhile, in 1969, Seale was indicted as a member of the 1968 "Chicago conspiracy," although he had spent only one day in the city during the Democratic convention. Bound and gagged during the trial, which turned into a personal and political confrontation between the judge and the defendants, Seale was sentenced to four years in prison for contempt of court by Judge Julius Hoffman. Seale then was tried in New Haven, Connecticut, for allegedly ordering the killing of a former Panther, but the jury was unable to reach a verdict, and the charges eventually were dropped.

So, by 1971, the three top Panther leaders were either in exile or faced possible prison sentences, and the party itself was divided.

And, in New York, 21 Panthers arrested in April 1969 for allegedly plotting to bomb a number of public buildings, went on trial finally in late 1970, after most of the defendants, held in $100,000 bail, already had spent more than a year in prison. The judge, it should be added, had been chosen by the District Attorney—the prosecutor!—and was well known for his pro-police sentiments. Indeed, as a public official, he once had been indicted for "overlooking" police graft.*

It was perhaps this record that prompted Yale president Kingman Brewster to say: "I am skeptical of the ability of black revolutionaries to achieve a fair trial anywhere in the United States."

Indeed, as the nation moved into the seventh decade of the 20th century, there was room for skepticism in most aspects of black–white relations in America. "There has been some progress, yes," one NAACP official said in July 1970, "but there is more resistance to Negro aspirations today than at any time in recent history."

This was true not only among private citizens but also

---

* The Panthers were acquitted in May 1971 despite what several jurors described as the trial judge's "bias" against the defense. Since most of the defendants were not able to raise the inordinately high bail, they spent, in effect, more than two years in prison for nothing!

within the government. "For the first time since Woodrow Wilson," said Bishop Stephen G. Spottsword, chairman of the board of the NAACP, "we have a national Administration that can be rightly characterized as anti-Negro." He cited as evidence President Nixon's nominations of Clement Haynesworth and G. Harrold Carswell to the Supreme Court, presidential aide Patrick Moynihan's memorandum calling for "benign neglect" of the race issue, and various Administration attempts to weaken civil rights legislation.

"In the final analysis," the U.S. Commission on Civil Rights noted in October 1970, "achievement of civil rights goals depends on the quality of leadership exercised by the President in moving the nation toward racial justice." But President Nixon's record leaves little hope that this leadership will be forthcoming. "The Federal Government is sanctioning racism," Julian Bond charged, "and black people can no longer look to it for assistance."

Where, then, can they look? With the government unsympathetic and most whites hostile, the avenues of peaceful protest appear to be closed off. "We're forced to become revolutionaries," says a forty-eight-year-old lawyer from Pontiac, Michigan, "since they program us right out of the system."

Where the black revolution will lead, no one can predict. "The young whites, and blacks, too," Malcolm said, "are the only hope that America has." And Cleaver said that if "a man like Malcolm X could change and repudiate racism, if I myself . . . can change, if young whites can change, then there is hope for America."

Martin Luther King, however, may have said it all when he warned: "Negroes hold only one key to the double lock of peaceful change. The other is in the hands of the white community."

Bibliographical Note

Of the many books I read in the course of my research, several were exceptional either for their writing, or their breadth, or their insights, or a combination of these qualities. Rather than make an exhaustive catalogue of my sources, I shall list these books below. An asterisk indicates that the book is available in a paperback edition.

Two excellent general books on reconstruction are: *The Era of Reconstruction*, Kenneth M. Stampp, New York, Knopf, 1965; and *Reconstruction After the Civil War*, John Hope Franklin, Chicago, University of Chicago Press, 1961.* Both are concise, objective and informative. For a more detailed account, with a Marxist orientation, see *Black Reconstruction*, W.E.B. Du Bois, New York, Harcourt Brace Jovanovich, 1935.*

A fine book on the postreconstruction years is: *The Betrayal of the Negro*, Rayford W. Logan, New York, Collier Books, 1954.* It examines Jim Crowism, northern as well as southern versions, in politics, the press, literature and art. Another good study of the period, but not as detailed, is *The Strange Career of Jim Crow*, C. Vann Woodward, New York, Oxford University Press, 1966.*

The leading black figure of this period was Booker T. Washington. I found no critical biography of him, but his autobiography, *Up from Slavery,* New York, Bantam Books, 1970,* is unwittingly revealing in its portrayal of a black man desperate to succeed in white America.

Washington's antithesis was W.E.B. Du Bois, the intellectual father of black militance. A good biographical study of him as a social propagandist is: *W.E.B. Du Bois*, Elliot M. Rudwick, New York, Atheneum, 1969.* Du Bois' *Autobiography*, New York, International Publishers, 1968*, is fuller and more wrathful, but curiously slack. A product of his last years, it appears in part to be an assemblage of excerpts from old speeches and documents. Much more poetic and concise, and containing many biographical insights, is his short study, *The Souls of Black Folk*, New York, Fawcett World, 1970.*

One of the best biographies of a black leader is the portrait of the flamboyant Marcus Garvey in *Black Moses*, E. D. Cronon, Madison, University of Wisconsin, 1955.* Sympathetic yet critical, it also is fully documented and well written.

A good journalistic account of the Movement's activities from 1954–1964, the Brown decision to the Civil Rights Act is: *Portrait of a Decade,* Anthony Lewis, New York, Random House, 1964.* The early years of SNCC, the most active and least institutional of the civil rights organizations, are well described in *SNCC: The New Abolitionists*, Howard Zinn, Boston, Beacon Press, 1964.* Mr. Zinn himself was active in many of the student protests.

There is not yet a balanced, incisive biography of Martin

Luther King, Jr., and King's own books are uneven. His first one is still the best: *Stride Toward Freedom,* New York, Harper & Row, 1958.* Besides telling the story of the Montgomery bus strike, it contains biographical material and a full explanation of King's concept of nonviolence.

In the case of Malcolm X, we are more fortunate; shortly before he died, Malcolm finished the brilliant account of his life: *Autobiography of Malcolm X,* New York, Grove Press, 1964.* It is unlikely that any biographer ever will produce a book as vivid, powerful and penetrating as Malcolm's own work.

Of the several studies of black nationalism, the most comprehensive and objective is: *Black Nationalism,* E. U. Essien-Udom, Chicago, University of Chicago Press, 1962.* The author deals with the political and cultural implications of black nationalism, concentrating on the Black Muslims. And for a provocative discussion of colonialism and African nationalism, see *The Wretched of the Earth,* Frantz Fanon, New York, Grove Press, 1968.* Fanon's theories have influenced most black nationalists in one way or another.

For an unflinching look at the problem of black identity in white America, see: *Soul on Ice,* Eldridge Cleaver, New York, Dell, 1968.* Cleaver's essays on black nationalism, Martin Luther King, Stokely Carmichael, Ronald Reagan, the Black Panthers and other related subjects have been collected in *Eldridge Cleaver: Post-Prison Writings and Speeches,* edited by Robert Scheer, New York, Vintage Books, 1969.* The pieces on the Panthers' confrontations with the police are especially eye-opening. For another sensitive account of the black man's travail in white Ameria, see *Soledad Brother: The Prison Letters of George Jackson,* New York, Bantam, 1970.*

INDEX

Abernathy, Ralph, 145, 148, 161
Addams, Jane, 79
American Colonization Society (ACS), 163–164
Ames, Adelbert, 44, 46
Armstrong, S. C., 67, 69

Baker, Ella, 119, 122
Baker, Ray Stannard, 64
Baldwin, John B., 26
Bell v. *Maryland,* 121
Black Codes, 23
Black, Hugo L., 112
Black Man, 171
Black Muslims, 103, 172–175, 177–180, 201
Black Panther Party, 103, 195, 199–203
  ten point program, 200–201, 203
Black power, 81, 103, 190, 192
Black Star Line, 168, 169
Black studies, 103, 197–199
Bond, Julian, 119, 207
Boutwell, Albert, 145
Boutwell, George, 30–31
Boycott, 137–141, 143
Brotherhood of Sleeping Car Porters and Maids, 98, 99
Brown, H. Rap, 196–197

Brown v. *The Board of Education of Topeka,* 105, 112, 114
Bullock, Rufus B., 70, 72

Cable, George W., 60
Carmichael, Stokely, 103, 191–196, 201
Carpetbaggers, 37–39
Carswell, G. Harrold, 207
Chaney, James, 125
Civil Rights Act of 1866, 16, 29
Civil Rights Act of 1875, 17, 45, 53, 56
Civil Rights Act of 1964, 103, 113, 125, 153–156
Cleaver, Eldridge, 103, 184, 201, 202, 203, 207
Cleveland, Grover, 72
Coleman Report, 113
Committee on Civil Rights, 100–101
Community Relations Service, 155
Congress of Racial Equality (CORE), 102, 103, 116–117, 119, 121–122, 124, 125–126, 144, 151, 190
Connor, Eugene "Bull," 128, 145, 146–147, 148
Coolidge, Calvin, 170

211

212 Index

Council of Federated Organizations (COFO), 124, 125
Crisis, 80, 81, 97–98
Cuffee, Paul, 164

Darrow, Clarence, 89
Davis, Angela, 203
Davis, Harry W., 11–12
Delany, Martin R., 164
Dixiecrats, 104
Domestic Marshall Plan, 91
Douglass, Frederick, 9, 13–14, 21–22, 26, 45, 46, 66, 74, 97, 115
Du Bois, W. E. B., 39–40, 72–73, 74–83, 169, 170

Economic and Youth Opportunities Agency (EYOA), 187
Economic Opportunity Act (EOA), 186
Eisenhower, Dwight D., 108–109, 114
Elijah Muhammad, 172–174, 177–179, 181–182
Emancipation Proclamation, 10
Equal Employment Opportunity Commission, 155
Essay on Civil Disobedience, 138
Evers, Medgar, 124, 126, 150

Fair Employment Practices Committee (FEPC), 99–100, 102
Farad, Wali, 173

Farmer, James, 102, 116–117, 121, 127, 151, 190
Faubus, Orval, 107–109, 111
Federal Bureau of Investigation (FBI), 108, 109, 131, 196(f.), 197, 202–203
Fellowship of Reconciliation, 116, 126
Fessenden, William Pitt, 28
Fifteenth Amendment, 16, 30–31
First International Convention of the Negro Peoples of the World, 169
First Reconstruction Act of 1867, 16, 33, 35
Fourteenth Amendment, 16, 30, 31, 33, 47, 53, 54, 112, 121
Freedmen's Bureau, 29–30, 34, 67
Freedom Democratic Party (FDP), 125–126
Freedom ride, 102, 126–131, 144
 "journey of reconciliation," 102, 126
Freedom Schools, 125
Fugitive Slave Law, 164

Gandhi, Mohandas, 116, 135, 142, 144
Garner, John Nance, 154
Garner v. *Louisiana,* 120–121
Garrison, William Lloyd, 19–20, 79
Garvey, Marcus Mosiah, 163, 165–171, 182, 197

Garvey's Watchman, 166
Goodman, Andrew, 125
Grandfather clause, 84
Grant, Ulysses S., 3–4, 20, 43, 44, 46

Hall v. *deCuir,* 53
Hamer, Fannie Lou, 124
Hampton Institute, 67–69
Harlan, John Marshall, 54, 55
Hayes, Rutherford B., 17, 47–49, 50, 51
Haynesworth, Clement, 207
Health Education and Welfare, Department of, 190
Heart of Atlanta Motel v. *United States,* 155–156
Hoffman, Julius, 203
Huckleberry Finn, 57
Humphries, Benjamin G., 26
Hutton, Bobby, 202

I Have a Dream, 125
Innis, Roy, 190

Jackson, George, 203
Jackson, Mahalia, 152
Jefferson, Thomas, 172
Jim Crow Laws, 51
Johnson, Andrew, 15, 16, 18–19, 23–29, 31, 34, 153
Johnson, Claudia Alta Taylor, 154
Johnson, Eliza McCardle, 24
Johnson, Lyndon B., 125, 153–156, 158
Julian, George W., 34, 44

Kennedy, John F., 111, 149, 150, 153, 154, 155
Kennedy, Robert F., 128
King, A. D., 149
King, Coretta Scott, 135–136, 139
King, Martin Luther, Jr., 102, 103, 122, 125, 132–144, 145–149, 152–153, 155–162, 179, 183, 189, 192, 207
King, Martin Luther, Sr., 133, 134, 143
Ku Klux Klan, 42–44, 88–89, 93, 107, 120, 170, 175
Ku Klux Act, 43

Lee, Robert E., 4
Letter from Birmingham City Jail, 145–148
Lewis, John, 102, 127, 191
Liberian Exodus Company (LEC), 164–165
Lincoln, Abraham, 8–15, 16, 18, 24, 27, 164
Lodge, Henry Cabot, 65

Malcolm X, 103, 175–182, 183, 184, 191, 197, 201, 207
March on Washington, 1963, 103, 150–153
March on Washington Movement, 96, 99, 100
Marshall, Burke, 149
Marshall, Thurgood, 85
Massive Resistance, 107
Matthews, Zeke T., 129
Maynard, Horace, 28
McCarthy, Joseph R., 82

214 *Index*

McDew, Charles, 119, 122
McKinley, William, 58, 63–64
McKissick, Floyd B., 151, 160, 190, 192
Meredith, James, 192
Montgomery Improvement Association (MIA), 139, 140–141
Moses, Robert Parris, 118–119
Moynihan, Daniel Patrick, 207
Muhammad Speaks, 179

National Advisory Council on Civil Disorders, 189
National Association for the Advancement of Colored People (NAACP), 79, 80, 81, 83, 84, 85, 89, 90, 91, 102, 105, 112, 116, 117, 119, 122, 124, 134, 135, 136, 183, 198, 207
National League on Urban Conditions among Negroes; *see* Urban League
National Negro Committee, 79
Negro Factories Corporation (NFC), 168
Negro World, 167–168, 171
Newton, Huey P., 103, 199–206
Niagra Movement, 78–79, 84
Nixon, E. D., 133, 137
Nixon, Richard M., 82, 207
Nonviolent resistance, characteristics of, 142–143
North American Aviation Company, 93–96

Office of Economic Opportunity (OEO), 186–187
Organization of Afro-American Unity, 180
Orr, James L., 26, 38
Ovington, Mary White, 79, 80, 84

Pan-African Congress, 81–82, 169
Pan-African Movement, 81
Parks, Rosa, 136–137, 139
Patterson, John, 128
Peck, James, 127
Person, Charles, 127
Peterson v. *Greenville,* 121
Phillips, Wendell, 10, 19–20, 23, 27, 29–30
Plessy, Homer Adolphe, 54
Plessy v. *Ferguson,* 54–55, 56, 106
Poor People's March on Washington, 160–161
Populist Party, 65–66, 93
Powell, Adam Clayton, 159

Rainey, Joseph, 36–37
Randolph, A. Philip, 96–101, 151
Rayburn, Sam, 154
Robinson, Jackie, 88
Roosevelt, Franklin D., 92, 93, 96, 99
Roosevelt, Theodore, 56
Russell, Richard, 154
Rustin, Bayard, 102, 127, 140, 143, 150–151

Scalawags, 37–39

Index 215

Schurz, Carl, 41–42
Schwerner, Michael, 125
Seale, Bobby, 199–201, 203
Sheridan, Philip H., 33
Shuttlesworth, Fred Lee, 145, 148, 149
Sit-in, 116–121, 126, 131, 144, 145
Sixth International Convention of the Negro Peoples of the World, 170
Southern Christian Leadership Conference (SCLC), 102, 122, 124, 143–144, 150, 158, 161
Southern Manifesto, 107
Southern Regional Council, 124
Southern Tenant Farmer's Union (STFU), 93
Spottsword, Stephen G., 207
Stanley, Thomas B., 106
Stephens, Alexander H., 26
Stevens, Thaddeus, 11, 19–21, 27–28, 33, 34, 44
Student National Coordinating Committee; *see* Student Nonviolent Coordinating Committee
Student Nonviolent Coordinating Committee (SNCC), 102, 103, 122–123, 124, 125, 126, 127, 128, 129, 131, 144, 151, 157, 158, 190–191, 195–197
Summer Freedom Project, 125
Sumner, Charles, 11, 14–15, 18, 20–21, 27, 33, 34, 44–45

Sweet, Ossian, 88–89

Talented Tenth, 75, 78
Talmadge, Herman, 106
The Messenger, 97–98
The Negro Is a Beast, 56
The Philadelphia Negro, 76
The Souls of Black Folk, 77, 96–97
Thirteenth Amendment, 10, 53, 54
Thoreau, Henry David, 138
Thurmond, J. Strom, 104
Tilden, Samuel J., 47–49
Trice, Jack, 62–63
Truman, Harry S, 100–101, 104
Turner, Henry MacNeal, 164, 165
Tuskegee Institute, 62, 69, 70, 72, 73

Uncle Remus, 57
Understanding clause, 58
Union League, 42
United States v. *Cruikshank,* 47
Universal Negro Improvement Association (UNIA), 167, 169–171, 175
Up From Slavery, 166
Urban League, 89–92, 102, 119, 122

Villard, Oswald Garrison, 79, 80
Vinson, Frederick M., 105

Index

Voter registration, 123–125, 126, 129, 144, 157
Voting Rights Act of 1965, 103, 158

Wade, Benjamin F., 11–12, 44
Wade–Davis Bill, 11–12
Waite, Morrison R., 47
Wallace, George C., 110–111, 157
War on Poverty, 184, 186
Warren, Earl, 105, 106, 121
Washington, Booker T., 66–73, 74, 77, 78, 132, 161, 166
Watson, Tom, 65–66
"We Shall Overcome," 122
Wells, Ida B., 63–64
White backlash, 158–159, 187
White devil, the, 174, 177
White, George H., 64
White primary, 58, 84, 105
White, Walter, 80–81, 85, 96, 99
Wilkins, Roy, 84, 85, 198
Wise, Stephen S., 79

Young, Whitney M. Jr., 90–91